The
Complete
Bar Writer

The Complete Bar Writer

Alexa Z. Chew
Katie Rose Guest Pryal

Carolina Academic Press
Durham, North Carolina

Library of Congress Cataloging-in-Publication Data

Names: Chew, Alexa Z., author. | Pryal, Katie Rose Guest, author.
Title: The complete bar writer / by Alexa Z. Chew, Katie Rose Guest Pryal.
Description: Durham, North Carolina : Carolina Academic Press, LLC, [2020]
Identifiers: LCCN 2020028378 (print) | LCCN 2020028379 (ebook) |
    ISBN 9781531017873 (paperback) | ISBN 9781531017880 (ebook)
Subjects: LCSH: Bar examinations--United States--Study guides. |
    Practice of law--United States. | Legal composition.
Classification: LCC KF303 .C44 2020 (print) | LCC KF303 (ebook) |
    DDC 340.076--dc23
LC record available at https://lccn.loc.gov/2020028378
LC ebook record available at https://lccn.loc.gov/2020028379

Carolina Academic Press
700 Kent Street
Durham, NC 27701
Telephone (919) 489-7486
Fax (919) 493-5668
www.cap-press.com

Printed in the United States of America

Contents

Online Materials

Additional content for *The Complete Bar Writer* is available on Carolina Academic Press's *Core Knowledge for Lawyers* (CKL) website.

Core Knowledge for Lawyers is an online teaching and testing platform that hosts practice questions and additional content for both instructors and students.

To learn more, please visit:

coreknowledgeforlawyers.com

Instructors may request complimentary access through the "Faculty & Instructors" link.

Preface

We wrote this book for law students and lawyers studying for the bar exam and for professors and other instructors helping people study for the bar exam.

The premise that underlies this book is this: the Multistate Performance Test (MPT) and the Multistate Essay Exam (MEE) are, at their core, legal writing exams. The legal writing skills that students learn in law school—and that students will need after law school when they enter law practice—are the skills they need to write well for the bar.

The more we studied the MPT and MEE, the clearer the relationship between **legal writing skills** and **test-taking skills** became.

Let us explain.

A. These Skills Are Important Skills

The purpose of this book is to teach readers legal writing skills that will serve them well on the MPT and MEE—and in law practice. The title of this book, *The Complete Bar Writer*, tells you that we intend to teach readers how to write well for the bar exam. But we will *also* show readers that learning to write for the bar exam is not a waste of time. Bar writing need not be a skill that test takers dump in the trash along with their test materials when they walk out of the bar exam.

No, the legal writing skills we teach in this book are skills readers will keep forever. In teaching terms, these skills are *transferable*. In fact, we connect the learning readers did in their first-year legal research and writing courses to what they need to know for bar writing, and then connect that new knowledge forward to legal writing in law practice. So much of students' knowledge can transfer. And, along the way, we help fill the gaps in readers' knowledge.

The MEE closely resembles a writing task that law students are already familiar with: their law school essay exams. **Both are legal analysis essays that use C-RAC structure.** Furthermore, like on the MEE, when students write their law school exams, they do not have legal authorities at their disposal.

The MPT more closely mimics a practical legal writing assignment. The client file is complete, the legal authorities have been pulled. Test takers must use their knowledge to figure out what writing task they must write (Office memo? Trial brief?), read the facts and law to formulate a legal analysis, and then write the legal document—all in 90 minutes.

Of course, we do provide many tips for how to do legal reading and writing under pressure, and tips for the bar exam in particular. However, fundamentally, most of the skills needed to do well on the bar exam are skills that you need to do well in any high-pressure legal writing situation.

That's a relief. That means studying for the bar exam isn't a waste of time. It'll make you a better lawyer.

B. Scope

This book covers two portions of the Uniform Bar Exam (UBE): the Multistate Performance Test (MPT) and the Multistate Essay Exam (MEE). Some jurisdictions that do not use the full UBE do still use portions of it: test-takers might encounter an MPT or an MEE or similar essay exam even if they are not in a UBE jurisdiction.

The MPT is the test that will be most foreign to law students, and we give it more attention in this book. Everything, from the test packet to the task assignment to how it is graded will be new and, frankly, weird. The MEE, on the other hand, will be more familiar, because the MEE questions resemble law school essay exams, just in shorter form. We give advice for how to complete the MEE, and pull back the curtain on the MEE itself, but because the MEE is far less complex than the MPT (and much shorter in duration), we do not focus as much of the book on specific strategies to complete the MEE.

However, there are many chapters in this book that help readers improve their performance on *both* tests. After all, to do well on the MPT and MEE, readers need many of the same skills. Therefore, we handle topics such as time management, writing under pressure, organizing legal analysis, evaluating practice tests, and more.

C. Three Governing Principles of This Book

There are three principles that guided us as we wrote this book.

Decide in Advance

When writing for the bar exam, you should decide as many things as you can in advance of test day. In this book, we encourage readers to make decisions now, to gain habits now, so that when test day comes, they do not have to make decisions that could have been made in advance. Here are some examples:

(1) Read the MEE prompts before reading the fact pattern.
(2) Complete MPT-1 before MPT-2.
(3) Memorize the MPT citation style so it is second nature.

There are many more choices that we encourage students to make, and many more good habits we encourage them to form, than the ones listed here. The point is this: preparation isn't just about memorizing the law for the MEE, for example. It's about learning good test-taking, legal writing, and lawyering skills before you need them under pressure.

The Bar Exam Is a Quirky Boss

As we were writing this book, we noticed lots of difficulties that both tests placed on examinees. We recognize that these difficulties can be frustrating. But we encourage readers to set aside their frustrations and accept the constraints of the test. They need to do so not only to succeed on the test, but also to succeed in the legal profession.

Throughout this book we refer to the MPT (and the bar exam) as a "quirky boss." Your quirky boss hands you a writing assignment, an incomplete case file, a ridiculously short amount of time in which to write a vague assignment—and then your boss goes out on a hike so you can't ask your boss questions.

What a horrible boss!

Except—as many of us know, we might encounter bosses just like this in legal practice. Sure, not all bosses will act like this all the time, but difficult situations do occur, and being able to roll with the difficulties and perform well under pressure will serve any lawyer well in practice. Ridiculous deadlines. Incomplete files. Confusing assignments. Hard-to-reach supervisors. Clients who can't get their facts straight or who have made really, really bad decisions—those are all part of law practice.

We encourage readers to think of the skills they're learning as **lawyering skills,** not just test-taking skills. The bar exam is a quirky boss, and test-takers have to make their quirky boss happy—just like the bosses they will have in the future.

Genre Discovery

The third principle that guided us as we wrote this book is genre discovery. **Genre discovery** is an approach for learning how to write unfamiliar genres, by which a writer studies samples of a genre to identify the genre's conventions so that she can write the genre.[1] A major benefit of this approach is that a writer doesn't need a mentor to give her instructions about how to write an unfamiliar genre. Instead, she can rely on her systematic study of sample documents. Once she discovers the genre's conventions, she can give herself instructions.

On the MPT, the exam assigns all kinds of writing tasks (or genres). Some tasks are tested frequently, like the argument section of a trial brief or a traditional office memo. Others have been assigned only once, like a legislative leave-behind, a genre that neither author of this book had heard of before reading that MPT.

There's no way to predict which genre the MPT will assign on a given exam, but you can learn a system that will help you no matter what genre you are assigned. That's what genre discovery is for.

The bar essays of the MEE is just another genre, one that many students have some familiarity with because it is like a genre they wrote in law school, their law school final exams.[2] This book teaches students how to transfer their knowledge from their law school exams and legal writing classes to the bar exam so that they can write strong MEE answers.

D. About the Complete Series

This book is part of The Complete Series for Legal Writers. The first, *The Complete Legal Writer* (Alexa Z. Chew and Katie Rose G. Pryal, 2nd ed. 2020), introduced the genre discovery approach, along with other foundational legal

---

1. Katie Rose Guest Pryal, *The Genre Discovery Approach: Preparing Law Students to Write Any Legal Document*, 59 *Wayne Law Review* 351–81 (2014). Dr. Pryal also owes a debt to her colleague and co-author Professor Jordynn Jack of the University of North Carolina at Chapel Hill, with whom Dr. Pryal worked closely on genre pedagogy for many years.

2. Law school exams are one example of a "student genre." Other examples of student genres from law school include research papers, response papers, reflection papers, student notes, and more.

concepts such as citation literacy. This book, *The Complete Bar Writer*, is the second in the series, and will be followed by *The Complete Legal Stylist* and *The Complete Legal Editor*.

The Complete Series for Legal Writers teaches legal research and writing concepts as transferable skills — as systems that readers can easily apply in a variety of unpredictable situations. To be complete does not mean to list every possible scenario, but rather to prepare readers to encounter them.

E. Acknowledgements

We would like to first thank all of the wonderful, loving people who cared for our children without complaint so that we could write this book. This care work too often goes unacknowledged. We are going to acknowledge it here and first: Karen, Yolany, Michael, Spanish for Fun Academy, Carol and Bob, Stefanie and Matt, Amy, Angelia, Beki, Christina, Eric, Jennifer, Kevin, Susan, Steve, Tyler, and more.

We would like to thank community organizations who support our work, including University of North Carolina School of Law who supported this book through research assistance and La Vita Dolce Café who supported this book through wonderful writing atmosphere and beverages.

Our colleagues at the University of North Carolina School of Law helped bring this book to life, including all of our colleagues in the Writing and Learning Resources Center: Craig Smith, Kevin Bennardo, Luke Everett, Patty Frey, Rachel Gurvich, Pete Nemerovski, Michela Osborn, and Sara Warf.

In particular, our colleagues Kaci Bishop and O.J. Salinas provided immense inspiration and editorial support for this project.

Aaron Kirschenfeld and Melissa Hyland of the UNC Law Library helped us with critical research for this book.

Mary-Rose Papandrea, Carissa Hessick, and Melissa Jacoby of UNC Law have been encouraging mentors.

We would like to thank the students of Professor Pryal's Fall 2019 Writing for the Bar course and Professor Bishop's Spring 2020 Writing for the Bar course, who used this book in an earlier form and helped us make it better. In particular, Ashle Page (UNC Law 2020) provided careful edits.

And a big thank you to Laura Johnson and Stephanie Long, Professor Chew's research assistants, who worked incredibly well and under time pressure to help make this book useful and readable.

The
Complete
Bar Writer

Chapter 1

How to Use This Book

If you are reading this book, then you are preparing to take the bar exam. Congratulations! You have already accomplished a lot by attending law school. Now you must pass the bar exam, and we will help you do so.

This chapter describes how to use this book, depending on your situation and needs. This book is designed to be read either from cover to cover or by reading only the chapters that will be most helpful to you.

A. Book Coverage and the Bar Exam

This book covers four main topics:

- The **Multistate Performance Test**, called the **MPT**.
- The **Multistate Essay Exam**, called the **MEE**.
- Test-taking strategies.
- Legal reading and writing under pressure, which are lawyering skills you will need to pass the bar exam.

Each jurisdiction's bar examiners determine the format and coverage of their bar exams. Some states use the **Uniform Bar Exam** (**UBE**), and some states use their own exam. Whether you are in a UBE jurisdiction or not, this book will be useful to you.

If your jurisdiction uses the UBE, you will take the MPT and MEE. All jurisdictions that use the UBE administer the same test in the same format to their examinees. The UBE has three components: the MPT, the MEE, and the Multistate Bar Examination (MBE), which is a 200-question multiple-choice test. If your jurisdiction uses the UBE, then this book will expressly address the writing components of your bar exam, the MPT and MEE.

Even if your jurisdiction does not use the UBE, this book will still be useful to you. First, your jurisdiction will use essay questions that are similar to the MEE. Because all bar exams include an essay-writing section, you'll benefit from the portions of this book that cover the MEE, test-taking strategies, and legal writing under pressure. However, you will need to figure out how those essay exams differ (if at all) from the UBE's MEE essays in order to adapt the techniques in this book to your jurisdiction's essay questions.

Furthermore, some non-UBE jurisdictions use the MPT or a similar performance test as part of their bar exam. If your jurisdiction does, then this book will expressly address how to take the MPT. If your jurisdiction uses its own performance test, similar but not identical to the MPT, you'll benefit from this book. As with non-UBE essay questions, you should figure out how your jurisdiction's performance test differs (if at all) from the MPT.

B. Making This Book Work for You

If you do not plan to read the entire book from front to back, you should strategically choose the chapters that will most help you reach your goal of passing the bar exam. You must figure out what your specific needs are.

Need: Strengthen Legal Reading, Reasoning, and Writing Skills

The MPT and MEE both require strong legal reading, reasoning, and writing skills. You might need to brush up on these skills. This book teaches these skills in Appendix 1, Legal Writing under Pressure, and Appendix 2, Legal Reading under Pressure. You should read these appendices if you need to brush up on your legal reading and reasoning or on your legal writing.

If you haven't written a practical legal document in a while, you should read Appendix 1, Legal Writing under Pressure, which covers basic legal writing conventions that apply to both the MPT and the MEE. The MPT only asks for practical writing, and it expects you to be able to follow basic legal writing conventions and compose an office memo, the argument section of a trial brief, and a letter. The MEE requires you to conduct basic legal analysis and follow basic legal writing conventions, particularly the C-RAC structure. Appendix 1 will teach you what you need to know to write organized MEE essays.

If it's been a while since you read law for the purpose of writing an analysis that solves a practical legal problem or an argument that supports a desired conclusion, you should read Appendix 2, Legal Reading under Pressure, which

🔥 Hot Tip

We refer to **C-RAC structure** throughout this book. C-RAC is one common acronym for the standard structure of legal analysis: conclusion, rule, application, and conclusion. Other common acronyms are IRAC, CREAC, TREAC, and CRuPAC. They all mean the same thing: first state the answer to your analysis's legal issue, then describe any applicable law, then explain how that law applies to your facts to support your conclusion. If you aren't sure what C-RAC is, read Appendix 1, Legal Writing under Pressure.

covers practical reading of primary legal texts and legal analysis, topics that apply to the MPT and might be helpful background for the MEE. For example, 3Ls who are used to reading law for the purpose of learning the law or answering questions in class might need to brush up on how to read law to use it to complete lawyering tasks. This is the kind of reading that practicing lawyers do and that first-year legal writing courses cover. If you're a practicing attorney, you probably don't need to brush up on legal reading.

Although the appendices focus on legal writing and reading skills that will serve you well during your legal career, in the appendices (and throughout this book) we provide tips that are targeted specifically to help you succeed on the bar exam.

And lastly, we recognize that reading and writing under immense professional pressure—and time pressure—is likely different than what you have experienced before. Appendices 1 and 2 will help improve your ability to read and write under intense time pressure.

Need: Learn How to Succeed on the MPT (or Other Performance Tests)

The MPT simulates the kind of writing lawyers do in practice. Therefore, when you take the MPT, you will write documents similar to the documents you wrote in your first-year legal writing courses, in law-school clinics, in the legal workplace, or on pro bono projects.

If you are taking the MPT, you should read these chapters:

- Chapter 2, What You Need to Know About the MPT, which describes the parts of the MPT exam, its purpose, how it tests, and how it is graded.
- Chapter 3, How to Take the MPT, which teaches you an effective method for taking the MPT called "genre discovery."

- Chapter 4, MPT Core Genre: Office Memo, which provides a detailed demonstration of genre discovery and familiarizes you with the core genre that the MPT tests most frequently, the office memo.
- Chapter 5, MPT Core Genre: Brief, which provides a shorter demonstration of genre discovery and familiarizes you with another core genre, the brief.
- Chapter 6, MPT Core Genre: Letter, which provides a shorter demonstration of genre discovery and familiarizes you with another core genre, the letter.
- Chapter 8, Evaluate Your Practice Tests, which helps you evaluate your practice MPTs so that you can improve your ability to write MPTs in the future.

Need: Learn How to Succeed on the MEE (or Other Bar Exam Essays)

The MEE essays most closely resemble your law school essay exams, except that they are designed to be written in thirty minutes: they are shorter and address a small number of legal issues. Like your law school exams, they test your knowledge of legal concepts, and they don't require you to cite particular cases or statutes. You are given a fact pattern to read and a legal question to answer.

If you are taking the MEE, you should read these chapters:

- Chapter 7, The MEE Bar Essays, which describes the MEE and provides strategies for taking it.
- Chapter 8, Evaluate Your Practice Tests, which helps you evaluate your practice MEEs so that you can improve your ability to write MEEs in the future.

Need: Test-Taking Strategies and Advice

The bar exam is a high-stakes test that most examinees find stressful. It's a test not only of knowledge and skill but also of endurance. If you're taking the UBE, you'll take the bar exam in four three-hour blocks of time over two days. If you receive extra time as an accommodation, you'll spend even longer than that.

If you have any qualms about succeeding on the bar exam, read these chapters:

- Chapter 9, Test-Taking Strategies, which provides strategies to help you prepare for the bar exam.

- Chapter 10, What If Things Go Wrong?, which helps you problem-solve, in advance, the possible challenges that might arise when you write for the bar.

C. Making This Book Useful beyond the Bar Exam: Testing, Lawyering, and Legal Writing

For all its shortcomings, the bar exam does indeed test important lawyering and legal writing skills. But because it does so in the context of a time-pressured test, you're likely focused on acquiring the important skill of **test-taking**. However, these three skills—test-taking skills, legal writing skills, and lawyering skills—work together to make you a stronger bar writer and a stronger legal professional.

You likely picked up this book because you want to pass the bar exam—that is, you want to know how to pass a test. When you read this book, however, you will learn more than test-taking skills. You will also learn **legal writing skills**. After all, the MPT and MEE are legal writing tests. You must have strong legal writing skills to pass them.

Moreover, you will also learn **lawyering skills**: professional skills that lawyers and other legal professionals need to succeed in their careers. These skills include following directions, managing time, meeting audience expectations, and completing tasks quickly.

Throughout this book, we will refer to these three sets of skills as we teach you how to succeed in bar writing. Each strategy or technique we teach you might be one (a test-taking skill) or two (a test-taking and a lawyering skill), or even all three.

But one thing is certain: you must develop strength in all three areas in order to pass the bar. No matter how strong your writing is, if you can't follow directions, you will not only frustrate your future employers, you will write an unsuccessful MPT.

Fortunately, this book will give you all you need to develop the necessary strengths to be a strong bar writer, no matter where you're starting from.

Chapter 2

What You Need to Know about the MPT

The **Multistate Performance Test** (**MPT**) is a test of practical writing skills created by the **National Conference of Bar Examiners** (**NCBE**). Many jurisdictions use the MPT on their bar exams, including every jurisdiction that uses the **Uniform Bar Exam** (**UBE**). The MPT simulates the kind of writing lawyers do in practice, so on the MPT you will write documents similar to the documents you wrote in your first-year legal writing courses, in clinics, in the legal workplace, or on pro bono projects. These documents include office memos, trial briefs, letters, and more.

On the Uniform Bar Exam, the MPT is actually two tests in one. You will receive a test packet that includes two separate writing assignments, your MPT-1 and your MPT-2. You have three hours to complete both tasks (or 90 minutes for each), and each task is (usually) a different document type. Thus, you might have to write an office memo and the argument section of a trial brief, or a trial brief and a client letter, or a demand letter and a contract, and so on. Each of the tasks uses entirely different facts and law. If you are taking the MPT as part of the Uniform Bar Exam, it counts for twenty percent of your total test score.

Note: Some jurisdictions that do not use the Uniform Bar Exam *do* use the MPT. Some of these jurisdictions only require you to complete one MPT, not both. California is an example of a jurisdiction that has had test-takers complete only one MPT.

This chapter will give you an overview of the MPT. Later chapters will give you specific strategies for how to complete MPT tasks.

A. What the MPT Tests

On the most basic level, the MPT tests three things:

(1) how well you can **read** a packet containing facts and law;
(2) how well you can **write** an assigned document type (called a "task") using those facts and that law; and
(3) how well you can do these things under a **time constraint**.

The NCBE, on its website NCBEX.org, states that the purpose of the MPT is to test "an examinee's ability to use fundamental lawyering skills in a realistic situation and complete a task that a beginning lawyer should be able to accomplish." That's great news! By the time you finish law school, you will be a beginning lawyer. Therefore, according to the creators of the MPT, you will have all the knowledge you need to take the test.

(However, if you feel shaky about any of these skills, you can check out Appendix 1, Legal Writing under Pressure, and Appendix 2, Legal Reading under Pressure.)

We agree with the creators of the MPT—you have the knowledge you need to take the test, even if you need to brush up on some things. What we will do in this book is help you hone your existing knowledge. We will also help you build your confidence so that you can focus on showing off your knowledge rather than worrying about the test itself.

But what law should you be studying to do well on the MPT? The NCBE states, "The MPT is not a test of substantive knowledge. Rather, it is designed to evaluate certain fundamental skills lawyers are expected to demonstrate regardless of the area of law in which the skills are applied." That's more great news. You don't need to study substantive law to do well on the MPT. You only need to study lawyering techniques, that is, how to read legal authorities and write practical legal documents.

To write practical legal documents under time pressure, you need expertise in various document types that lawyers write. Another word for "document types" is "genres." The MPT will assign you a genre to write—your task—and you will have to write it as efficiently as possible.

Most of the time, the MPT tests genres that are likely familiar to you—like memos, briefs, and letters. We call these the "core" MPT genres. The MPT also tests genres that might be unfamiliar to you, such as drafting documents (e.g., contracts and wills) or judicial documents (e.g., opinions and bench memos). We call these the "rare" MPT genres. This book will give you an approach for writing *any* genre that the MPT might present to you, core or rare.

B. The MPT Is Your Boss

Other bar exam guidebooks encourage you to think of the MPT as a difficult code that needs breaking, as a test that needs "hacking." But we believe this mindset is a waste of your valuable time and energy. The MPT, in the end, is testing skills that you already have and that you will need later in practice. You don't need to be a hacker or a code-breaker to succeed on the MPT. You just need to adapt your existing legal writing and lawyering skills to writing your MPT tasks.

Think of the MPT as a quirky boss. This quirky boss has specific ways that it wants its documents prepared, and this boss has given you only certain materials to use. Your quirky boss has also given you only a short amount of time in which to complete your task.

These constraints on your writing might feel frustrating or unrealistic.

They aren't. You will have quirky bosses throughout your legal career. If you've spent much time in the workplace, chances are you've had a quirky boss already. Quirky bosses are normal. They do things like give you last-minute assignments. Or incomplete case files. Or odd organizational demands for their legal documents. We, the authors of this book, have experienced these quirks throughout our own legal careers. In fact, as we write this list, we're wondering if we should even call this behavior "quirky." It just sounds "boss-like."

The MPT is your boss, and you have to do what your boss tells you to do in order to score well on the MPT. If you accept this test-taking premise, the MPT no longer seems like a weird game. It starts to seem like the thing that the bar examiners intended: a test of your practical legal writing skills.

And if you accept that you will encounter quirky bosses (and judges and opposing counsel) when you enter the legal profession, you will develop an important lawyering skill.

C. How the MPT Tests

On test day, you will receive your stapled packet of two MPTs, called MPT-1 and MPT-2. You won't be allowed to separate the pages. Having to flip around in a 40-page stapled booklet is a limitation that you should know about, and practice using, in advance. At the beginning of the test booklet will be a single table of contents for both MPT-1 and MPT-2.

Each MPT itself is divided into two parts: the **file**, which contains your task memo and the facts of your case, and the **library**, which contains the law. Also contained in the file are any other documents that will help you understand your task: templates, instructions, and samples. We refer to these, along with the task memo, as "task documents." Be prepared to identify your task documents right away when you first open your MPT. Your task documents help you understand your quirky boss, which will help you accumulate more points on the MPT.

Your MPTs will use both state and federal law, but they will use fictional jurisdictions—the fictional states of Franklin, Olympia, and Columbia, along with the fictional federal 15th Circuit. Be prepared to see these fictional jurisdictions when you open your library. Also be prepared to see real federal law, like provisions from the United States Code or abridged versions of U.S. Supreme Court cases.

The MPT tests your proficiency in writing certain tasks. These tasks are legal genres: office memos, briefs, letters, contracts, and so on. Sometimes, one MPT task document will require you to write *two* tasks: a main task and another task that explains the main task. We refer to the second, explanatory task as an **add-on**. An example of an MPT task that includes an add-on might be a contract revision (the main task) and then an office memo to explain your revisions (the add-on).

In writing this book, we studied past MPTs and counted how frequently these genres were tested on the MPT. We looked at thirty-two MPTs given over the seven-year period prior to the writing of this book (2012–2019) and categorized them by genre and frequency. The data appears in Figure 2.1.

Figure 2.1. Genres on the MPT

Name of Genre	Number of Appearances
Office Memo	10
Brief	9
Letter	7
Add-On Office Memo	2
Judicial Document (Bench Memos)	2
Contract (Drafting)	1
Corporate Document (Drafting)	1
Legislative Document (Drafting)	1

Our research shows that the office memo, the brief, and the letter are by far the most commonly tested genres. Moreover, every add-on assigned from 2012–2019 was an office memo. Because of how frequently the MPT assigns the office memo, the brief, and the letter, we call these the **core MPT genres**. With respect to briefs, between 2012 and 2019, the UBE has only assigned trial briefs (not appellate briefs). Furthermore, when it has assigned trial briefs, it has only assigned the argument sections. Although appellate briefs and trial briefs have many similarities, you need to become confident writing trial briefs.

The rare genres during those years were bench memos and drafting genres like contracts and proposed legislation. It is not possible to list every rare genre that the MPT might give you to write. But that's okay. We don't need to list them, and you don't need to learn to write them. Instead you'll use what this book teaches you about the core genres and interpreting task documents to write any genre the MPT throws at you.

Thus, you need to be able to write the three core MPT genres—office memo, brief, and letter—before you take the MPT. Based on the numbers, you're very likely to be asked to write an office memo, and you're pretty likely to be asked to write a brief or a letter. Moreover, rare tasks are often variations or combinations of office memos, briefs, and letters.

You also must be able to write the core MPT genres with confidence because the MPT is unlikely to provide detailed instructions (or any instructions) for how to write them. The MPT does, however, provide instructions for how to write the rare MPT genres. Thus, you'll need to be able to rely on your memory to write an office memo, brief, or letter. Just as you need to memorize black letter law to succeed on other parts of the bar exam, you will need to memorize the basics of the core genres.

And just to be clear, you do not need to write a perfect legal document on the MPT. In your legal writing course or while working, you might have developed some specific and high standards for an office memo, brief, or letter. Perfection is not the goal on the MPT. Displaying competence is. You'll gain this competence through practice and evaluation, which in turn will make you feel confident.

If you don't yet feel confident writing office memos, briefs, and letters, Chapters 4, 5, and 6 of this book teach you how to write them. Pair those chapters with Appendix 1, Legal Writing under Pressure, which will help you improve your writing skills when writing under pressure. You also must practice what you have learned and review your practice MPTs. Chapter 8, Evaluate Your Practice Tests, teaches you how to effectively evaluate your practice MPTs.

D. How MPTs Are Graded

MPTs are graded by attorneys in each jurisdiction, not by a central grading authority. They are graded quickly, usually in just a few minutes. In other words, this task you will spend ninety minutes writing will only be given three or four minutes of a grader's attention.

The NCBE gives each jurisdiction's graders a grading tool called a "point sheet." A point sheet is a narrative description of how the NCBE expects the document to look (i.e., the parts of the document) and the legal points that the document should make. These legal points include rules, application of law to specific facts, conclusions, argument headings, contract clauses, and so on.

The point sheet, despite its name, does not tell the grader how many numerical points to assign to each part of your task. Instead, it describes how an ideal version of your task should be written. Individual jurisdictions determine how to assign numerical points to your MPT answers. It is highly unlikely that you will ever know how those points are assigned, either before or after you take the bar exam.

In Chapter 8, Evaluate Your Practice Tests, we describe how to use point sheets to help you study for the MPT. You can view actual point sheets at the end of sample MPTs you download from the NCBE website.

🔥 Hot Tip

> Learning that graders only spend a few minutes on your exam might frustrate you, but it also provides an opportunity. In the legal profession, you will encounter busy readers: judges, senior partners, and more. They will skim your writing rather than read it carefully. You will need to learn to write in such a way that it can be skimmed and still understood: this is not only an important **test-taking skill** for the MPT but also an important **legal writing skill**.

E. Take a Practice MPT Right Now

Before you go any further, you must take a practice MPT. You can download past MPTs for free from NCBEX.org.

When you practice an MPT, you should practice under test conditions. There are three things you should try to imitate: the exam software you will use, the writing implements you will have, and the time constraints you will face.

Exam Software: To imitate your exam software, use the focus mode in Microsoft Word[1] or the similar function in the writing software of your choosing. Focus mode removes all of the formatting choices and other features from your computer screen, more closely modeling exam software.

Writing implements: All jurisdictions limit what you can bring into the test room with you, but some jurisdictions are extremely restrictive. For example, North Carolina does not allow you to bring in any writing implements. Instead, it provides every examinee with an identical set of pens, pencils, highlighters, and erasers. Learn ahead of time what writing implements you can use on test day, and practice with them. If you are taking the bar exam in a jurisdiction that does not allow you to bring any of your own writing implements, don't get attached to one particular style of pen or pencil. When you practice, practice with the pens you will likely use when you take the test.

Time Constraints: When you practice the MPT, use a timing device, and be strict about time. Time pressure is a major factor on the MPT, and you should mimic it when you practice. Sometimes, you should practice under a time constraint that is shorter than you will have on bar exam day: 75 minutes, for example. This added time pressure will make the full 90 minutes seem much easier.

Now, go take a practice MPT. We're serious. The rest of this book will not be nearly as useful to you if you do not. You're going to have to take practice MPTs anyway, so go ahead. Take one now.

F. The MPT Materials

Congratulations! You just took your first practice MPT. Let's review the test packet you received and compare it to the packet you will see on test day. The purpose of this section is to familiarize you with the MPT materials to help you avoid surprises. On test day, familiarity is your friend. As you read this section, you should have a printed sample MPT by your side, such as the MPT you just took.

---

1. To use focus mode in Microsoft Word, go to the "View" menu, then select "Focus." (These instructions might not work with your version of the software. If they do not, you can look up the instructions on the internet.)

The Test Packet

On test day, you should get acquainted with your test packet as quickly as possible so that you can start reading and writing immediately. In UBE jurisdictions, your MPT test packet contains both MPTs you are required to take, labeled MPT-1 and MPT-2. Each is supposed to be a 90-minute test. However, you will have a three-hour block of time during which to take the entire MPT. It is up to you to ensure that you use your time wisely. (In some jurisdictions, you only have to take one MPT or similar practice test.)

The Instructions

On test day, when you receive your test packet, it will be sealed. You cannot open it until you are instructed to do so. While you are waiting, flip it over. On the back will be instructions. If you have time to read the instructions before the test begins, then you should read them. If you do not have time to read the instructions, don't worry about it. The instructions typically do not change from year to year; therefore, read the instructions carefully on your practice MPTs.

On your practice MPT that you have downloaded, the instructions do not appear on the back—they appear after the table of contents, preface, and description. When you practice, practice like on test day: skip to the instruction page and read them first.

The instructions state that you are not allowed to remove pages from the test booklet as you work. The test booklet contains both of the MPTs that you will take, all bound together into one large packet. Be prepared for this presentation of the test because it can feel unwieldy to have all of the materials stapled together and to be unable to separate them.

If you separated them when you took your first MPT, that's okay. Just remember you can't do it when you take practice MPTs in the future.

The MPT Jurisdictions

The instructions contain information about the jurisdictions of the MPT. The MPT is set in a fictional state jurisdiction (usually a U.S. state called Franklin) or in a fictional federal jurisdiction (usually the 15th Circuit). Neighboring fictional states of Olympia and Columbia are often referenced in the legal authorities. The state courts of Franklin are, in order, the District Court, the Court of Appeal, and the Supreme Court.

The fictional jurisdictions can be surprising, so prepare yourself for them. When you took your practice MPT, were you surprised by these jurisdictions?

Did you wish you had known about them in advance? The more familiar you can make the test, the better.

The Table of Contents

After you open the packet on test day, you will find the **table of contents** (**TOC**) that covers both of your MPTs, MPT-1 and MPT-2. The parts of each MPT are the "file," which contains the task memo and the facts of your case, and the "library," which contains the law.

The TOC will describe in detail which fact documents and legal authorities are contained in each MPT. Thus, the TOC can give you valuable information about your MPTs. Glance at the list of legal authorities that you will be reading for each problem. Most MPTs give you a selection of law in a grouping that you have likely seen before when doing legal writing, e.g., a group of cases, or a statute with cases interpreting the statute. However, sometimes, the law in the library is unusual; you will want to know that in advance.

On your practice MPT, the TOC likely included the point sheets listed at the bottom. The point sheets are the grading guide sheets that the graders receive. When you are taking a real MPT, you will not receive the point sheets.

The Preface and Description

In the practice MPT that you downloaded, you will receive a preface to and description of the MPT. These do not appear on the real MPT. Following these pages are the instructions to the MPT, but you have read these already.

Now that you have taken a practice MPT and are familiar with the MPT's purpose and the packet, let's dive into how to take the test.

Chapter 3

How to Write the MPT

The purpose of this chapter is to give you an approach for taking any MPT, no matter what that MPT's task, facts, or law might be.

This book's approach to the MPT is called "genre discovery." Genre discovery is a process for learning how to write legal genres that are unfamiliar to you. On the MPT, genre discovery is a **test-taking skill**: it teaches you to draw upon your prior knowledge about practical legal writing and combine it with the test materials so that you can write your MPT task.[1] Genre discovery is also an effective **legal writing skill** that you can take with you after the MPT.

Genre discovery on the MPT has four steps:

(1) Identify your MPT task name.
(2) Identify your audience and purpose.
(3) Create an outline for how to write your task (what we call a "schematic").
(4) Add law and facts to your schematic and complete your task.

Let's learn the approach that will help you write any task you encounter on the MPT.

A. About Genre Discovery

The MPT assigns writing tasks for you to complete. These writing tasks are document types, such as "memos" and "letters." Another word for a document

---

1. The essays of the MEE are also a genre, similar to the final exam essays that you likely wrote in law school. Therefore, they are a genre that is somewhat familiar to you. (In other ways, the MEE is unlike your law school exams. You will learn more about the MEE in Chapter 5 of this book.)

type is "genre." A genre is a recurring document type that has certain predictable conventions. For example, an office memo is a document type that recurs—that is, happens over and over again—because lawyers frequently write them.

Conventions are the parts of a genre and the ways that audiences expect a genre to be written. In this way, conventions are the "rules" of a genre.[2] Continuing our example, conventions of an office memo include a question presented and a brief answer. These don't always appear in an office memo—but they often do, and if you were to see a document that contained them, you would recognize the document as an office memo.

Why would you recognize the office memo? (Or appellate brief, or contract?) Because legal genres are standardized forms for presenting legal information. When a legal supervisor assigns you a writing task, your legal supervisor will call that task by its name, say, "demand letter." If you are a new lawyer in a firm, you might have a conversation like this:

> **Supervisor**: Please write a demand letter to opposing counsel for $10,000 to settle the case.
> **You**: Sure.
> [Supervisor leaves.]
> **You**: [To yourself.] What's a demand letter?

In this example, your supervisor has asked you to write a document that you are unfamiliar with, something you weren't taught to write in law school. However, from this short conversation you can tell that a "demand letter" is a genre because your boss referred to it as something she presumed you both would be familiar with. This presumption of familiarity shows that the genre preexists your conversation—that it exists among lawyers. And if a genre exists, then you can discover it.

When discovering genres in the workplace, you usually have a lot of resources available to you. Those resources include your boss, peers, sample documents you can find in client files, your employer's guidelines for how to do things, reference books, the internet, and your prior knowledge. Using these resources, and focusing specifically on the samples, you determine the conventions and write the document you were assigned.[3]

But sometimes you will not have all of these resources, like if you work in a solo practice. Another time is when you take the MPT.

---

2. These definitions of "genre" and "conventions" are from *The Complete Legal Writer*. See Alexa Z. Chew and Katie Rose Guest Pryal, *The Complete Legal Writer* (2nd ed. 2020).

3. Alexa Z. Chew & Craig T. Smith, *Border-Crossing: Genre Discovery and the Portability of Legal Writing Instruction*, 25 Perspectives 8 (2016), bit.ly/chew-smith.

Just like the rest of the legal profession, the MPT uses legal genres when it assigns writing tasks. When the MPT assigns you a task to write, it is assigning you a genre to write. But, as you learned in Chapter 2, the MPT is also a quirky boss, which means that the MPT sometimes refers to tasks using task names that aren't commonly shared among lawyers. The MPT task names can be confusing. That's one challenge of having a quirky boss like the MPT.

Another challenge of this quirky boss is that you can't ask it for sample documents (also called "go-bys" by lawyers) to write your task. Sometimes the MPT gives you a sample, but most of the time it doesn't. When you take the MPT, you can't ask your boss questions—imagine that your boss has given you an assignment and then has gone on a hike in the woods without cell phone service. Plus, you have a really tight deadline.

Essentially, when you write your MPT task, you can imagine you are working in a firm under time constraints with very few resources. The MPT, then, is a great way to practice for tough situations in law practice. And you *will* encounter tough situations.

◊ Hot Tip

Doing genre discovery in *any* resource-limited, time-stressed legal situation is a **legal writing skill**. Doing it on the MPT is a **test-taking skill**. Although it might take you a couple of practice MPTs to get the hang of this process and to customize it to your style of writing, once you have the hang of it, your test-taking (and legal writing) speed will increase.

B. Your Genre Discovery Resources on the MPT

On the MPT, you will have two types of materials to conduct your genre discovery: the MPT task documents and your prior knowledge of legal documents.

Your Task Documents

When you receive your MPT packet, the test materials will be divided into two parts: the "file," which contains the task memo and your client's facts, and the "library," which contains your legal authorities.

Some of the documents guide you in writing your task. We call these "task documents." Your task documents are (usually) located at the beginning of the file of your MPT packet. Task documents include the following:

- **Your task memo.** You might have encountered documents similar to a "task memo" in real life, but with different names such as "assigning memo," "assignment," or simply "memorandum."
- **Any guidelines the MPT gives you.** Sometimes these guidelines include a template.
- **Any sample documents the MPT gives you.** Sometimes these sample documents can be found among the legal authorities in the library.

Merely reading the task memo is not enough to learn how to write your task. You do need to read the task memo, but you also need to read all of the other task documents—if the MPT provides any beyond the task memo. As a general rule, the MPT provides less guidance for the core genres (office memo, brief, and letter) and more guidance for rare genres. Chapters 4, 5, and 6 give more information about the core MPT genres.

It is your job to figure out which materials are task documents and, combined with your prior knowledge, use them to do genre discovery.

Your Prior Knowledge

The MPT, and this book, presume that your prior knowledge includes confidence in writing three core legal genres: the office memo, the brief, and the letter. The MPT will give you fewer task documents for the core genres because it presumes you have more prior knowledge of them. Therefore, before taking the MPT, you should be a confident writer of all three core genres.

🔥 Hot Tip

> Confidence in the three core genres is not only a required **test-taking skill**, but also a required **legal writing skill** for the workplace. If you are not confident, you must become so. Chapter 4, MPT Core Genre: Office Memo, Chapter 5, MPT Core Genre: Brief, and Chapter 6, MPT Core Genre: Letter, teach you how to write them. Pair those chapters with Appendix 1, Legal Writing under Pressure, which will help you improve your writing skills when writing on a tight deadline with few resources. You also must practice what you have learned. Therefore, download past MPTs to practice with from the NCBEX website, and use the techniques you learn from this book to practice.

On the MPT, you may also encounter genres beyond the office memo, brief, and letter. These genres, such as the contract or will, may be unfamiliar to you. This chapter, along with the MPT demonstrations in Chapters 4, 5, and 6, show how to use genre discovery to write rare genres.

What do you do with your prior knowledge about your task? That's where genre discovery comes in. Let's review the four steps of genre discovery, and then walk through them together.

(1) Identify your MPT task name.
(2) Identify your audience and purpose.
(3) Create an outline for how to write your task (what we call a "schematic").
(4) Add law and facts to your schematic and complete your task.

Note: We are presenting these four steps in a linear fashion. As you become more proficient in taking the MPT, you will probably execute these steps more simultaneously. We will point out places where the steps overlap below.

The rest of this chapter will teach you how to do genre discovery on the MPT and then give you an opportunity to try it out on sample MPT task documents.

C. Identify Your Task Name (Step 1)

The first step in using genre discovery to complete your MPT task is to identify your task name.

Your task name is located in your task memo. When you come across what looks like a task name, immediately circle it with your pen or pencil. Here are some examples of real MPT task names from recent MPTs:

- "memorandum"
- "argument section of our brief in support of our motion for summary judgment"
- "opinion letter"
- "persuasive brief"
- "bench memorandum"

MPT task names can be tricky. Some of them mean exactly what you think they mean, and others don't. Two task names that mean what they say are "argument section of a brief" and "demand letter." If you see one of those task names, then you'll be writing what you think of as an argument section of a brief or a demand letter.

The word "memorandum," in particular, does not give you much information about what you are supposed to write. If your task name is "memorandum," then you might be writing an office memo, or you might be writing a bench memo or an interpersonal memo or even a motion memo.

When you're provided with a vague task name such as "memorandum," in order to figure out what kind of task you will be writing, you need to work through the next steps of the genre discovery process.

Except for demand letters (as we mention above), the different types of letters that you could be asked to write might not match up with what you think they mean. For example, you might have learned that a client letter should present a neutral legal analysis to your client. But on the MPT, the task memo's description of a "client letter" might be to convince your client to take a particular action. What the term "letter" does indicate, however, is that the design of your document is going to look like a letter, that is, if you saw the document at a distance, you would recognize it as a letter of some kind. But the purpose of that letter will be unknown until you study the task documents to identify the document's audience and purpose.

D. Identify Your Audience and Purpose (Step 2)

After determining your task's name and learning whatever you can from that ("I'm writing the argument section of a trial brief!" or "I'm writing a thing that looks like a letter!"), you need to identify your task's audience and purpose. Doing so will give you more information about the vague task that you might have been presented with.

Audience

At the time of this printing, the NCBE's "MPT Skills Tested" document states that the MPT tests your ability to "assess the perspective of the recipient of the communication."[4] Indeed, your ability to write well for your particular legal audience is not only critical to your success on the MPT, it is also critical to your success as a lawyer. In other words, the reason the MPT tests your ability to write for a specific audience is because lawyers must also do so.

For the MPT, you can think of your audience as falling into two general categories: expert and lay. "Expert" refers to members of the legal profession, and

---

4. National Conference of Bar Examiners, *MPT Skills Tested*, 2014, available at http://www.ncbex.org/dmsdocument/54.

"lay" refers to people who are not members of the legal profession (sometimes called "laypeople"). This division relies on these major assumptions: experts are familiar with legal concepts and terminology, and laypeople are not. These assumptions help you decide whether to use legal terminology without explaining it (for experts) or to explain any legal terminology that you use (for laypeople).

Your task memo will probably describe your audience. And if it doesn't, another task document (like a "guidelines" memo) will. Expert audiences include judges, opposing counsel, and clients who are described as lawyers. Lay audiences include anybody who is not obviously a lawyer.

⬥ Hot Tip

> If your audience is lay, the task documents probably specify that you should tailor your document to a non-expert audience. However, be careful because they might also specify that you include conventions that a lay audience wouldn't make much sense from, like legal citations.
>
> Also, when taking the MPT, you will encounter tasks in which the client is also a lawyer. In those situations, your audience is expert even though your audience is your client. Do not assume that every client is lay.

And, of course, you are writing for the graders of the MPT.[5] The MPT is graded by members of the bar of your state (not by a central agency). Grading the bar exam is a pretty thankless task that people take on because they care about people becoming lawyers. Graders often have a lot of exams to grade in a short period of time, giving each MPT only a few minutes, so it is important to make it as easy as possible for them to give you a good grade. The strategies in this book focus on making your answer easy to read so that you can earn as many points as possible.

---

5. For more discussion about bar graders as a legal writing audience, see Kaci Bishop and Alexa Z. Chew, *Turducken Legal Writing: Deconstructing the Multi-State Performance Test Genre* (on file with authors, abstract available at https://papers.ssrn.com/sol3/papers.cfm?abstract_id=3596148).

🔥 Hot Tip

In the legal profession, you will encounter busy readers who will skim your writing rather than read it carefully, including judges and senior partners. You will need to learn to write in such a way that it can be skimmed and still understood: this is not only an important **test-taking skill** but also an important **legal writing skill**.

Purpose

Knowing the purpose of your MPT task (or any legal writing task) tells you the *why* of your assignment. If you don't know why you are writing, you cannot write well. You can think of the purpose of legal documents as falling into two categories, what we call "analysis-to-conclusion" and "conclusion-to-analysis."

In **analysis-to-conclusion** documents, when you begin to write, you do not yet know the conclusion of your analysis. The purpose of your document is to use legal analysis to determine that conclusion for your audience. In other words, the document has a question that needs answering. An example of an analysis-to-conclusion document is an office memo. In an office memo, a supervisor asks you to find the answer to a legal question and support that answer with legal analysis.

In **conclusion-to-analysis** documents, when you begin to write, you already know the desired conclusion of your analysis. (The conclusion might have been given to you, say, by a legal supervisor.) The purpose of your document, then, is to use legal analysis to prove that conclusion to your audience. In other words, the document has a conclusion that needs proving. An example of a conclusion-to-analysis document is a trial brief. In a trial brief, you must prove to a judge that she should agree with the conclusions that are most beneficial to your client.

Figure 3.1. Analysis Terms Table

Analysis to Conclusion	Conclusion to Analysis
Question Needs Answer	Conclusion Needs Proof
Predictive	Advocacy
Objective	Persuasive
Neutral	Argumentative

These two purposes of legal analysis resemble terms used to categorize legal writing that you might have encountered before. We find that these other terms are less useful descriptions of purpose, but looking at these other terms can help connect your new knowledge to what you already know.

Practice Identifying Audience and Purpose

Now that you know what audience and purpose are, let's practice identifying them using examples from past MPTs. Below are three excerpts. Each excerpt comes from an MPT task memo assigned to examinees by a fictional supervising attorney. Read through each excerpt and, as you're reading, look for clues about the task's audience and purpose. Once you reach the end of each excerpt, note whether the audience is expert or lay, and whether the purpose is analysis-to-conclusion or conclusion-to-analysis. Then, check your answers against the explanation that follows each example.

Excerpt 1: "Please prepare an objective memorandum for me analyzing these questions...."[6]

Explanation 1: The task name is "objective memorandum." The task memo came from your supervising attorney, who asked you to write the memorandum for "me"—referring to herself. Because the audience of the memorandum is your supervising attorney, a member of the legal profession, your audience is expert. Your task memo instructs you to "analyze" some "questions" for that legal expert. These clues tell you that the purpose of this task is to answer a question. Thus, this is an analysis-to-conclusion task.

Excerpt 2: "Please draft a letter to [client] for my signature analyzing the legal consequences to [client's company] if...."[7]

Explanation 2: The task name here is "letter." The audience of the letter is a client who is not a member of the legal profession and is therefore lay. Your task document instructs you to "analyz[e] the legal consequences to" the client's company "if" an event comes to pass. The word "if" tells you that the conclusion of the analysis is unknown, which means this is an analysis-to-conclusion task.

Excerpt 3: "I am preparing a motion for preliminary injunction.... Please draft the argument section of our brief in support of the motion for preliminary injunction."[8]

Explanation 3: The task is "the argument section of our brief in support of the motion for preliminary injunction." The audience of the brief isn't stated. However, you probably inferred that the audience is a trial judge because that is usually who hears motions. If you turn the page in this MPT, you will find your "guidelines" document. The first sen-

---

6. National Conference of Bar Examiners, Multistate Bar Exam, July 2017 MPT-2.
7. National Conference of Bar Examiners, Multistate Bar Exam, February 2012 MPT-2.
8. National Conference of Bar Examiners, Multistate Bar Exam, July 2012 MPT-2.

tence reads: "The following guidelines apply to persuasive briefs filed in support of motions in trial courts." These guidelines confirm that your audience is a trial court judge, a member of the legal profession. Therefore, your audience is expert. Regarding purpose, because the brief is in "support of" a motion made before a trial judge, your brief aims to convince the judge to agree with your brief's conclusion that your client should win. Thus, this is a conclusion-to-analysis task.

As you read your MPT task documents, circle any clues about audience and purpose *as you read*, the first time you read. These clues will help you create your schematic, and circling as you read will save you time.

Now, using the task name, audience, and purpose, you can write your schematic.

E. Create Your Schematic (Step 3)

The next step in genre discovery is to create your schematic. In ordinary usage, a schematic is *a diagram of a complex idea*. Your schematic will guide you through completing your task, including how you read the rest of the file and the library and how you type your answer.

You will create your schematic in layers, adding to it as you read your test packet. You'll type your first layer directly into your exam software after reading enough of your task documents to identify your task. Then you'll add layers as you read your file and library. (Chapters 4, 5, and 6 model this process and show how a schematic develops, layer by layer.)

As you read your task memo, you may learn enough to immediately start typing your schematic into your exam software. You will then layer onto your schematic the new knowledge you gain about your task as you read more of your task documents. The point is, you don't have to be certain of everything about your document to start typing document parts that you already know.

◊ Hot Tip

It might feel weird at first to start typing before you have read your entire test packet. But starting to type your schematic immediately after reading your task memo is crucial to increasing your test-taking speed. You are creating a living outline of your MPT task that you can add to as you learn more about the task (if there are additional task documents) and read the facts and the law. When you read the facts and law, your schematic will give you a place to put that information. Furthermore, when you create a schematic, you avoid having to flip back and forth to the task documents as you read the later documents.

As you read your task documents, in addition to noting your task's name and your task's audience and purpose, mark any words that tell you what your document should look like or how you should write it. These are your task's document features. Here are three common categories of document features:

- The names of **parts** of your document, like "brief answer" or "conclusion."
- The **order** in which those parts should appear, including any omissions like "do not include a separate statement of the facts." (Leaving out the statement of facts is common on the MPT.)
- **How to write** those parts, like "your analysis should include headings" or "weave" facts and law.

After you finish reading your task documents, you'll add this new information about document features to your schematic. But that's not all the information that will go into your schematic. For the core MPT genres—office memos, briefs, and letters—you will add your prior knowledge about those genres to the schematic. The MPT rarely gives guidance about how to write office memos, and the guidance it gives about briefs and letters is minimal. That's why it is so important that you have confidence in writing the core genres. Your prior knowledge will provide the features that you default to in order to write your schematic for these tasks.

With rare MPT genres, your MPT task documents will provide more information about what your document should look like and how to write it. Occasionally, your MPT will even provide a sample.

Once you finish reading and annotating your task documents, you are ready to create your schematic. Type the schematic directly into your exam software. Most of the words in your schematic will become part of your MPT answer.

Add Headings for the Parts of Your Document

First, type in **headings for document parts**. Use both your prior knowledge of any core MPT genres and any explicit instructions in your task documents to identify the headings your document parts require.

- For an **office memo**, type the names of the generic office memo parts—Question Presented, Brief Answer, Factual Background, Analysis, and Conclusion.
- For the **argument section of a brief**, type "Argument" at the top of your document.

- For **letters**, you might not type anything because letters usually do not have headings for their parts. Of course if your quirky boss told you in your task memo to write headings for some parts of your letter, type them first.
- For any rare MPT genres, type in whatever parts your task documents describe.

Ensure that your headings are in the **correct order** on your page. If your task documents say to omit particular document parts (like a statement of the facts in an office memo), **include the heading** but write [omitted], in brackets, beneath the heading. Leaving in the heading and writing [omitted] will **show the grader that you know the correct document parts and headings of the genre.** It will have the added benefit of reminding you that you are not supposed to write the document part.

Write Known Parts Immediately and Write Placeholders for the Other Parts

Next, type any parts of the document that you can fill in based on the information in the task documents. Typically, these are document parts that take less than 30 seconds of thought.

For example, if you're writing a letter, you can immediately type the sender's name and address, recipient's name and address, the date, the greeting, the sign-off, and the signature block.

For document parts that you can't write immediately because you need to read the file and library and think about them, add **placeholders**. For a letter, you might start the first paragraph with, "My name is Ross Boss and I represent Cleo Client." And then you'll add to the rest of the paragraph once you learn more. You could also leave an extra large space in the middle of your letter document to show where the body of the letter—the part that will contain all of your legal analysis—would go.

Add Explicit Guidance

Add in any explicit guidance you find in the task documents about how to write your task. For example, your task memo might tell you to add certain features, like this: "Divide your analysis with argument headings in the form of complete sentences that combine law and fact to state a conclusion." If so, you should either draft conclusion headings based on your task documents or add placeholders for them. (For more about writing conclusion headings, see Appendix 1, Legal Writing under Pressure.)

Furthermore, guidance about how to write your task could also include a particular way to **structure your analysis**—say, "address each of these three issues separately." If so, you *must* follow that structure, even if it's not a structure you would have chosen for yourself. The MPT is your quirky boss, and you must do what your quirky boss says regarding the structure of your document.

◊ *Hot Tip*

> If you know your core genres well, then you know that you should use conclusion headings (another term for argument headings or point headings) to divide the different issues or sub-issues in your office memo or to divide the different arguments or sub-arguments in your brief.

Add Placeholders for the Rest

Finally, add in placeholders for any other items you know you'll need to write. For example, if your task is a brief, then you know you'll need to write C-RACs in the argument section. You can add placeholders for "rule," "application," and perhaps "addressing counterarguments."

Before you finish typing the first layers of your schematic, ensure you included *everything* from the task documents that will guide your writing. One goal of creating a schematic is to avoid having to flip back and forth to the task documents in your packet. If you don't know where to type something (like [include citations]), type it at the top of your schematic and keep going.

◊ *Hot Tip*

> If you aren't sure what C-RAC is, read Appendix 1, Legal Writing under Pressure. C-RAC is one common acronym for the standard structure of legal analysis: conclusion, rule, application, and conclusion. Other common acronyms are IRAC, CREAC, TREAC, and CRuPAC. They all mean the same thing: first state the answer to your analysis's legal issue, then describe any applicable law, then explain how that law applies to your facts to support your conclusion.

Once you've completed the first layers of your schematic, you're ready to read the rest of the file and the library, add more layers to your schematic, and efficiently write your answer.

Remember: the first time you use task documents to write a schematic, it might take a while. After all, you are learning a new skill. After you practice taking MPTs using this method, writing the schematic will go quickly.

F. Add Law and Facts to Your Schematic and Complete Your Task (Step 4)

After preparing the first layers of your schematic, you have essentially created a to-do list for your task. You have all of the parts laid out in your exam software. Now, you must read the facts and law to figure out how to fill in those parts and complete your task.

You have a choice to make: do you first read the facts (the portion of the file that follows your task documents), before you read the law (the library)? Or do you read the law before the facts? You should practice each way and decide which way works best for you. You may also find that one way works better depending on the characteristics of each MPT you're given. For example, for MPTs with short files and long libraries, reading the file first might work best for you. But if the MPT has a long file and a short library, reading the library first might work best for you.

Choice 1: Read the Facts First

Here is why it can be helpful to read the facts first. First, you have already done the kind of practical legal writing the MPT is testing. In the past, when doing practical legal writing, you have read the facts first. Only after reading the facts have you sought law to help you solve the legal problems generated by your facts. We are willing to bet that you have never, in the past, read law before the facts of the case when analyzing a legal problem for practical legal writing.

You should put your prior experience to use when you take the MPT. You should not create a new mode of legal writing simply for the MPT. Doing so is inefficient and could be ineffective, especially on test day when you will feel pressure and need to rely on trusted habits.

Moreover, after you pass the bar, you will read facts, spot legal issues, and then conduct legal research to help you solve legal problems. After you pass the bar, we are willing to bet, you will never read the law first before reading your clients' facts. You will not do this because it is not how lawyers do lawyering.

When you read the facts first, make notes with a pen or pencil of any facts that jump out as possibly relevant to your legal issue. If any seem obviously part of your analysis, type them into your schematic in an appropriate place. You might also type the page numbers on which those facts appear so they will be easy to return to.

Choice 2: Read the Law First

However, the MPT is a test. It has one significant difference from real life that makes reading the law first a good choice: **the MPT contains very little law when compared with real-life legal writing.** For this reason, many students find it helpful to read the law before the facts.

The task documents, which you'll have already read before you need to make this choice, likely contain enough facts that you can issue-spot when you read the law even if you haven't read the rest of the facts yet. Furthermore, like in all practical legal writing situations, the file contains more facts than are relevant to your legal analysis.

But, unlike in practical legal writing situations, the library only has a small amount of law, nearly all of which you are supposed to use in your analysis. The law on the MPT is tightly edited, so if you read it first, you will not be wasting your time reading extra law.

As you can see, there are good reasons to read the facts first and to read the law first. Plus there are good reasons to use one or the other depending on the particular MPT you are taking.

Law Library

The law library will contain fictional law from fictional jurisdictions, but the library may also contain real law, e.g., a real federal statute. However, sometimes an MPT will modify a real statute, so even if you are familiar with the area of law tested, you should presume that a legal authority is fictional and not rely on your prior expertise. In short, presume that all of the law in an MPT is fictional law.

Before you begin reading the legal authorities, flip through them so you can get a sense of their length and the order in which they appear. As you flip through the library, notice each authority's weight relative to the rest—courts generally must follow statutes, and lower courts must follow higher courts.

When flipping through cases, skim any citations within them to see if the authorities reference one another. Some examples:

- Newer cases might explain or apply older cases.
- Cases might explain or apply statutes.

Cases also might explain or apply cases that are *not in your packet.* Note, however, that these cases-within-cases are part of your library. In legal practice, you should *not* rely on cases that you haven't read—many practitioners consider doing so to be unethical, and you risk getting the law wrong.

But the MPT is a quirky boss who expects you to **use those cases-within-cases, even though you haven't read them.** You can rely on the information in those cases-within-cases as though you'd read the underlying cases yourself.

As you read the legal authorities, take notes based on your schematic and the facts you have read. Use a pen or pencil, not a highlighter. Annotate carefully, and a lot—you want to be able to easily find where things are. If you locate a rule or case example that you know you will need, go ahead and type it into the proper place in your schematic. Be on the lookout for legal tests: factors, elements, and the like. These will likely be important to your legal analysis.

As you type law into your schematic, be sure to type a citation right away—you do *not* want to have to go back and locate citations later.

MPT Citations

Plan to include citations for any law you write about in your task. Sometimes task memos or guidelines will instruct you not to include citations, in which case follow that direction. But otherwise, **cite after every statement of law just as you would in practice.** (Only rarely does the MPT expect you to cite to *factual* documents.)

Although the MPT expects you to include legal citations, it does not expect full *Bluebook*-style formal citations. You cannot do *Bluebook*-style citations because you do not have all of the information to do so—for example, cases in the MPT library do not have reporters or page numbers. Instead, you should **take your citation cues from the library of the MPT itself.** Model your citations on the ones you see in your packet. Here are some examples of citations from real MPTs:

Butte County v. 105,000 Square Feet of Land (Fr. Ct. App. 2005).

State v. Schmidt (Fr. Sup. Ct. 2003).

In the Matter of Devonia Rose (Olympia Sup. Ct. 2004).

Olympia Rule of Professional Conduct 8.4(c).

On the MPT, case citations include only the case name, the court abbreviation, and the year; the final two appear in parentheses. There are no volumes, reporter abbreviations, pages, or pin cites. Odd as this citation form might look, it does make some sense because the parenthetical information is enough to determine the case's weight: jurisdiction, court level, and recency. For statutes and regulations, follow the same strategy: mimic the citations you see in the library.

As in practice, after you've cited an authority once, you can use short form citations. Here are some example short form citations from real MPTs:

Butte County.

Id.

Rule 8.4(c).

Remember the most important rule of legal citation: make sure your reader knows which authority you are referring to. If you don't have time to format your citations with italics or perfect internal punctuation, that's okay, because your reader will still know what authority you are referring to. If you are taking the MPT and forget entirely how to write the citations, look at the authorities cited in the packet and mimic those citations.

Use Your Schematic to Finish Writing Your Answer

Writing your answer—completing your task—is the final step in genre discovery. Use the outline and notes in your schematic to finish writing your answer. You'll use your pre-existing knowledge of the core genres and basic legal writing conventions like C-RAC structure to turn your schematic into a document with sensible sections, paragraphs, and sentences. Chapters 4, 5, and 6 include sample MPT answers for the office memo, brief, and letter genres.

G. Practice Genre Discovery

Now it's time for you to practice doing the first three steps of genre discovery using a set of task documents to create a schematic. After you have given it a shot, we'll show you how we used those same task documents to start our schematic.

Figures 3.2 and 3.3 (below) contain task documents that we created to mimic an MPT: a task memo along with a memorandum containing guidelines. Using these documents, follow the steps of genre discovery to create the first layers of a schematic. Remember to annotate the task documents as you read them. Your annotations will help you quickly find the information you need to create your schematic.

After you finish annotating your task documents and creating your schematic, compare your annotations and schematic with ours. The last part of this section walks you through the categories of annotations and the process of creating the schematic.

Figure 3.2. Sample Task Memo

Gerber, Castellino, & Windham
Attorneys at Law
1201 Felix Street
Franklin City, Franklin 33206

To: Examinee
From: Belinda Bok
RE: Tony Chen
Date: July 28, 2020

My friend Tony Chen has consulted me about a problem he is facing with a family member passing stolen checks from his checking account. I offered our firm's services to help him solve his legal problem.

Tony travels out of the country frequently for work. He loaned his nephew, Joseph, his checkbook to pay Tony's utilities while he was in Hong Kong for work for two months. Tony gave Joseph permission to use the checkbook to pay only the utility bills and nothing else.

Joseph paid the power bill, the water bill, and the telephone bill using checks from the checkbook. However, while Tony was in Hong Kong, Joseph got behind on his own utility payments. He used Joseph's checkbook to make a payment on his electric bill, and then, using the last check, he purchased a new washer and dryer for his apartment.

Worse, after using those checks, Joseph did not have enough checks to pay for Tony's utilities and Tony's water was shut off.

When Tony returned from his travels, he was shocked to see the large purchases that had been made with money from his checking account and to discover turning his water back on would cost Tony $500. He came to me for help with two legal questions:

1. Can Tony sue Joseph and recover the money Joseph used to pay Joseph's electric bill and to purchase the washer and dryer?

2. Can Tony sue Joseph and recover the money Tony must pay to have his power turned on again?

Please draft an opinion letter to Tony for my signature, advising him on each of these issues. Please follow the firm's guidelines for opinion letters.

Figure 3.3. Sample Memo Containing Guidelines for Letters

Gerber, Castellino, & Windham
Attorneys at Law
1201 Felix Street
Franklin City, Franklin 33206

MEMORANDUM

To: Associates
From: Partners
RE: Opinion Letters
Date: January 1, 2012

Follow these guidelines when writing opinion letters to our firm's clients.

(1) Identify each issue separately. Present each issue as a question that can be answered with a "yes" or a "no."

(2) Following each question, give a brief answer that explains why the law and facts work together to provide that answer.

(3) After the question and brief answer, provide a fuller legal analysis of each issue in which you provide rules and citations, weaving together law and facts to explain your conclusions.

(4) Remember that most of our clients aren't lawyers, so avoid legalese. We want our clients to be able to understand our advice.

Annotations

Great job! Now let's review your annotations. Here is a list of the important things that you should have noted to make your schematic. If you didn't note all of these things, go back and find them. More practice will make it easier for you to spot these items in the future and to do so quickly. Plan to take many practice MPTs.

Task name

In the final paragraph of the task memo, you see that the task name is "opinion letter." The "letter" is one of your core genres, and now you know that your completed document will look like a letter and use the typical parts of a letter.

Audience and Purpose

The main audience clue is in the final paragraph: "to Tony." You know from the first paragraph that Tony Chen, the client, is a friend of your boss. There is no indication that Tony is a legal expert. Indeed, the guidelines document states that "most" of the firm's clients aren't legal experts. Therefore, for this task, your audience is lay.

You can find clues about the purpose throughout the task memo. In paragraph 1, you see that the client is "facing" a "problem," and he needs help "solving" it. These words tell you that the document is likely going to answer a question, and therefore it is an analysis-to-conclusion. There is another clue in the final paragraph: the word "advise." Nowhere does your boss give you the outcome or the conclusion. You must figure that out on your own.

Document Parts

The task memo is not the only task document for this MPT. The final paragraph refers you to your firm's guidelines for opinion letters. Turn to that document, and you will find explicit instructions for how to structure your letter. Here are some of those instructions:

- "Identify each issue separately" in the form of a yes/no question.
- "Give a brief answer."
- Give a "fuller legal analysis of each issue" in which you "weave together law and facts."
- "Provide citations."

What core genre does this structure resemble? An office memo.

Thus, although you will use the parts of the letter genre to design your document, you will also use some parts of an office memo because the guidelines tell you to do so. But beware: read through the list of guidelines again and see if you can spot what major part of an office memo is missing.

There is no summary of the facts on the guidelines. The guidelines include only issues, short answers, and analyses. There is no facts section, which is a standard office memo part. Also missing is the conclusion section. The point is, do draw on your prior knowledge, but also read the guidelines carefully.

When writing a letter to a layperson, you should ordinarily avoid citations. But these guidelines explicitly tell you to use them, so you should use them.

Writing Instructions

In the guidelines, there are also clues about how to structure your analysis. You are supposed to "identify each issue separately" and "provide a fuller legal analysis of each issue." What this means practically is that after you have identified your legal issues, you should analyze those legal issues with separate C-RACs because the guidelines require it.

What are your legal issues? They are the numbered questions on the task memo. Your task memo has given you an analysis structure.

Why do you have to follow the analysis structure given? Remember, the MPT is a quirky boss that insists you use its analysis structure. You will possibly encounter quirky bosses in legal practice, and you will have to follow their rules. Don't fight it, just do it. You will save yourself a lot of mental anguish on this test and in your legal career. Importantly, even if the authorities in the MPT library give you a different analysis structure from the one given in your task documents, use the structure of the task documents.

What about instructions that sound like advice, rather than mandatory instructions? Like this: "Weav[e] together law and facts to explain your conclusions."

If you read this statement on its own, it looks like writing advice—and indeed, that's what it is. You don't need writing advice from the MPT. You need information about your task and its rules. But you do need to be able to distinguish writing advice from mandatory instructions so that you can mentally set aside the writing advice. To review how to write strong legal analysis, however, see Appendix 1, Legal Writing under Pressure.

After you finish writing your schematic, see Figure 3.4 to compare your schematic with the one we created. Then, to see sample schematics along with completed tasks for the core MPT genres, read Chapter 4, MPT Core Genre: Office Memo, Chapter 5, MPT Core Genre: Brief, and Chapter 6, MPT Core Genre: Letter.

Figure 3.4. First Layers of Schematic for Your Letter Task

Gerber, Castellino, & Windham
Attorneys at Law
1201 Felix Street
Franklin City, Franklin 33206

Tony Chen
[Address Needed]

July 28, 2020

Dear Tony:

Thank you for trusting me to help figure out a strategy for responding to your stolen check problem. This letter contains my advice about whether you can recover funds from your nephew for his unauthorized purchases and for the money you paid to the water utility.

ISSUES:
1. Can Tony sue Joseph and recover the money Joseph used to pay Joseph's electric bill and to purchase the washer and dryer?

2. Can Tony sue Joseph and recover the money Tony must pay to have his water turned on again?

SHORT ANSWERS:
1. YES/NO. Tony CAN/CAN'T sue Joseph and recover the money Joseph used to pay Joseph's electric bill and to purchase the washer and dryer.

2. YES/NO. Tony CAN/CAN'T sue Joseph and recover the money Tony must pay to have his water turned on again.

ANALYSIS:
Funnel.[9]

I. YES/NO. Tony CAN/CAN'T sue Joseph and recover the money Joseph used to pay Joseph's electric bill and to purchase the washer and dryer.

Law

---

9. For more about how to write a strong analysis section, see Appendix 1, Legal Writing under Pressure.

Application

II. YES/NO. Tony CAN/CAN'T sue Joseph and recover the money Tony must pay to have his water turned on again.

Law
Application
Thank you for trusting me with your stolen check issue—I hope we can get together under better circumstances soon.

Sincerely yours,

Belinda Bok

Chapter 4

MPT Core Genre: Office Memos

This chapter has two purposes. First, the chapter will familiarize you with the core genre that the MPT tests most frequently: the office memo. Second, the chapter will model step-by-step how to take an MPT using the genre discovery technique you learned in Chapter 3, How to Take the MPT.

A. The Typical Office Memo

In general, an office memo is a document that a lawyer uses to convey her analysis about a legal question. The reader is usually a legal supervisor. Often, office memos are written by junior attorneys to senior attorneys in response to a research assignment. Senior attorneys often ask junior attorneys to write office memos to help the senior attorneys prepare to counsel clients. Office memos should explicitly assess strengths and weaknesses of the conclusions that their writers draw. This kind of balanced, neutral assessment helps the senior attorney make sound decisions and give useful advice to the client, even if it's advice that the client might not want to hear. Because the office memo is an analysis-to-conclusion genre, they are sometimes referred to as "objective memoranda."

Below is an annotated description of a typical office memo. Office memos, like any genre, vary depending on audience and purpose. But if you don't already have a description of an office memo in your memory, use this one.

Annotated Description of an Office Memo

These four lines at the top of the memo are called a caption.

On the MPT, your name is just "Examinee."

To: Your audience, usually a supervisor
From: You
Date: The date
Re: A brief description of your memo's topic, often including client name and legal issue

Use all-caps to label document parts because bar exam software has limited formatting capabilities. If you can center your part headings, do so. If not, don't worry about it.

MPT office memos typically have two or three issues.

QUESTIONS PRESENTED

I. This is a legal question that you have been asked to answer. Questions presented are usually one sentence long, reference both law and fact, and end in a question mark. A question presented is the same thing as an "issue." You need one question presented per issue.

II. A second question presented, if needed.

BRIEF ANSWERS

I. A short answer to the question presented. Begin with a one- or two-word answer (yes, no, probably, probably not). Then, in one-to-three sentences, summarize the key law and how it applies to your facts.

II. Each question presented should have a matching brief answer.

On the MPT, you will often be instructed to omit the facts section of your office memo. If so, write the part heading and then [omitted] beneath it, as in the sample that follows.

C-RAC is covered in more detail in Appendix 1, "Legal Writing under Pressure."

STATEMENT OF FACTS

Describe the legally relevant facts of your case. Present them chronologically and in enough detail that your reader will be able to follow the story and will not be surprised by new facts in the Analysis section of your memo. Use paragraphs to divide the story into logical parts.

ANALYSIS

The Analysis (or Discussion) part of your memo contains your legal analysis—the relevant law and how it applies to your facts to support a conclusion. The Analysis is composed of C-RACs.

Funnel: The first passage contains rules that apply to the whole Analysis section, organized from the most general to the most specific. We call this a "funnel" section. Not every Analysis will have a funnel. If your Analysis has a funnel, end the funnel with a roadmap, a sentence that summarizes the major conclusions of your Analysis. Not every Analysis needs a roadmap.

I. Write a conclusion heading for each issue. These headings should be complete sentences that state the conclusion of your analysis of that issue (the C of your C-RAC). ◄——— *You might see this style of heading referred to in the task documents as a "point heading" or "argument heading."*

Rules: Write the rules that apply to the facts of your case, including examples. Also include rules and examples that weaken your conclusion. Present the rules from most general to most specific, with examples typically last. Use legal citations. ◄——— *On the MPT, use the informal citation style that the MPT requires and that we teach in Chapter 3, "How to Take the MPT."*

Application: Apply the law from your "rules" section to the facts of your case. Divide your application into paragraphs as necessary, applying last any rules that weaken your conclusion (sometimes called counteranalysis).

II. Heading stating the conclusion of your second issue.

Rules: More rules here, like above.

Application: More application here, like above.

CONCLUSION

Briefly restate your overall conclusions. You can likely borrow from your brief answers and point headings.

B. Variants of the Office Memo Genre

The office memo also comes in different forms: variants of the genre that do different jobs depending on the audience and purpose of the document.

On the MPT, you may see these variants:

- **Office memo add-ons.** Sometimes an MPT task will have two tasks: the primary task and an add-on office memo. For example, you might be asked to modify a contract, and then to explain the modifications in a memo. Or you might be asked to write a client letter, and then to explain what you wrote in a memo.
- **Bench memo** or **bench brief.** A bench memo resembles an office memo. The audience of a bench memo is a judge, and the writer of the memo is a judge's clerk or other employee. The purpose of a bench memo can be either analysis-to-conclusion or conclusion-to-analysis. If you determine that your bench memo's purpose is analysis-to-conclusion, then your answer will be quite like an office memo. But if your bench memo's purpose is conclusion-to-analysis, then your answer might look like an office memo at a glance but read like a brief.
- **Some letter genres.** Sometimes the MPT specifies "letter" as a task but the instructions end up describing what is essentially an office memo, including the question presented and brief answer. Other times, the letter closely resembles an office memo but doesn't use all of the document parts. Watch out for these office memos masquerading as letters.

C. Office Memo: Genre Discovery

Now let's use excerpts from MPT task documents to do genre discovery of an office memo. If you need to review genre discovery, read Chapter 3, How to Take the MPT.

Imagine a sample MPT file,[1] one that contains two documents. The first is a typical "task memo" from your supervising attorney, a quirky boss named

---

1. This genre discovery demonstration and the sample schematic and answer that follow all refer to MPT-1 from July 2014. If you can, download the July 2014 MPTs and read along as we discuss it here. As of this printing, this MPT was available to download for free from the NCBE website, NCBEX.org.

Steve. The second is a letter from Steve's client, Kay, that details what she wants from Steve. The file does not include a separate sheet with guidelines for the document Steve wants you to write. Nor does it include any samples. The two-page letter from Kay is also the only factual document in the MPT, and it is both a factual document and a task document.

At the beginning of the task memo, Steve tells you that Kay is an attorney who has hired him to determine whether modifying "her current retainer agreement" with existing clients "to require arbitration of fee disputes" would be ethical and legally enforceable. The second paragraph of the task memo describes legal authorities that Steve has gathered for you (and that are included in the library), including the relevant Rule of Professional Conduct and two Franklin Court of Appeals cases.

The third and fourth paragraphs of the task memo describe your task. Steve tells you that he has a meeting scheduled with Kay in the coming week during which he will give her advice about the issues she raised in her letter. He needs you to help him prepare for the meeting and requests that you "draft a memorandum to me responding to her request for advice as communicated in her letter. Your memorandum should include support for your conclusions with citation to legal authority, taking care to distinguish contrary authority where appropriate."[2]

He then gives you some more advice about the document he wants you to write in the following paragraph:

> I think it is possible—from both an ethics and a legal enforceability perspective—to modify her retainer agreements to require arbitration of fee disputes, but only if certain conditions are met. Be sure to set forth those conditions in your memorandum.[3]

Let's use this information from the task memo to study the genre and begin writing our schematic. To review, here are the four steps of genre discovery you learned in Chapter 3:

(1) Identify your MPT task name.
(2) Identify your audience and purpose.
(3) Create an outline for how to write your task (what we call a "schematic").
(4) Add law and facts to your schematic and complete your task.

---

2. July 2014 MPT-1 File page 3.
3. July 2014 MPT-1 File page 3.

Task Name

Quirky boss Steve tells you that he wants you to "draft a memorandum" to him that responds to client Kay's request for advice. Thus the task name you are given is "memorandum." There aren't any other descriptions of what parts this memorandum should include or adjectives to describe the memorandum, like "objective." This is fine. The MPT sometimes provides tasks names like "memorandum" that don't have a clear meaning.

We need to study the audience and purpose to determine whether this memorandum is an office memo, another analysis-to-conclusion genre, or a brief that is wearing an office memo costume.

Audience and Purpose

The main audience clue is the phrase "to me" in the task memo excerpt, in which the author of the task memo tells you that the memorandum is for him. Who is "me"? The name in the "From" line of the task memo: Steve, your supervisor.

You need to determine whether Steve is an expert or lay audience. You can tell that Steve is an expert audience because the task memo says that he was "retained" by Kay, which identifies him as a lawyer. (Generally, your supervisor on the MPT will be a lawyer.)

The purpose of the memorandum, according to the same task memo, is to help Steve prepare for his upcoming meeting with Kay. To this end, Steve wants you to draft a memorandum for him that responds to Kay's "request for advice as communicated in her letter." A "request for advice" suggests that that your memorandum will be an analysis-to-conclusion document (as opposed to a conclusion-to-analysis document). Although Kay's desired outcome is to be able to add mandatory arbitration clauses to her retainer agreements, she wants to know if doing so would be ethical and enforceable.

At this point in your analysis of the task, you know that you are writing an office memo.

However, Steve has also told you that he thinks it is possible to modify Kay's retainer agreements to include mandatory arbitration clauses—but only if certain conditions are met. In a way, Steve has given you the conclusion: yes, it is possible to make the modifications that Kay wants. This information doesn't mean that your task is actually a conclusion-to-analysis document. If it were, then you would see persuasion language in the task document, words like "convince" and "persuade." It does suggest that the right answer will be "Yes, she can modify the retainer agreements but only if she meets the following conditions: [list the conditions]."

Clues about Document Parts

To begin creating our schematic, we'll want to know the typical parts of an office memo and how to write them. And we also need to closely examine the task documents for clues about document parts so that we can tailor our schematic to our quirky boss's specific requirements.

The task memo says nothing about including or omitting certain parts of a typical office memo. Thus, the MPT is assuming that you know how to write an office memo and what parts go into it. This is an example of how the MPT expects you to know the office memo genre before you take the test.

At this point, we have enough certainty that we're writing an office memo that we can begin writing our schematic. First, we'll type in the caption because that takes less than 30 seconds of thought. And then, we'll type in headings for the other parts of the typical office memo: question(s) presented, brief answer(s), facts, analysis, and conclusion. Those six parts will be the first layer of our schematic. If later we get instructions to the contrary, we can always adjust.

Schematic Layer 1. Office Memo Parts

To: Steve Ramirez
From: Examinee
Date: July 30, 2014
Re: Modification of Retainer Agreements

QUESTION PRESENTED

BRIEF ANSWER

FACTS

ANALYSIS

CONCLUSION

A schematic is a living document that you will add to as you read your file and library. The next section will demonstrate how to add layers to the schematic we started after reading the task memo.

D. Add Layers to Your Schematic

Often, the task memo will tell you everything you need to know to analyze the task's audience and purpose. But in this particular task memo, Steve refers multiple times to Kay's letter and hints that it contains more specific directions for you. So we should be prepared to add to those directions when we read Kay's letter. Kay's letter is also the only other document in this particular MPT file. There are no more factual documents. So once we've read Kay's letter, we've finished reading the facts as well.

Kay's letter repeats the general request for advice that was in Steve's task memo, provides some background about her solo law practice, and quotes the mandatory-arbitration sentence that she would like to add to her retainer agreements with existing clients. She also explains that her ultimate goal is to "see fee disputes resolved quickly and with a minimum of costs" to her and her clients.

Clues about Analysis Structure

Her letter also includes requests for advice on two issues, and her wording is more specific than the wording Steve used in the task memo. Nevertheless the gist is the same as what Steve told you and confirms that we are writing an office memo that addresses two issues: (1) What does Kay need to do under the rules of professional conduct to ethically modify her retainer agreements with current clients to cover future fee disputes? (2) How, if at all, does Kay need to revise her proposed language to be legally enforceable?

From this information, we know we can add these two issues to our schematic, along with any other information we learned from Kay's letter, like important facts from Kay's case. Often, "memorandum" task memos explicitly say, "do not draft a separate statement of facts." This one does not, so we can assume that we should write a separate statement of facts if time allows. Given how few facts there are, drafting a facts section should not take long.

Let's pause here for a moment and consider why we should follow Kay's implied two-part structure rather than reading the law, determining the test(s), and structuring our analysis based on the test. That's normally how lawyers structure their analyses, right? What if you read the law and find out that the applicable test has three parts, not two? Wouldn't it make more sense to structure your analysis around three issues rather than two?

Maybe! But it doesn't really matter. Remember that the MPT is your quirky boss, and sometimes bosses tell you to do quirky things that you don't agree with, like structure your memo around two issues **even when the legal test has three prongs.** You will possibly encounter quirky bosses in legal practice (or quirky judges), and you will have to follow their rules. Don't fight it, just do it, particularly on the MPT, a situation in which you cannot negotiate with your quirky boss.

So it's settled, we'll have an analysis with two issues. Let's add another layer to our schematic that shows where we'll address each issue and includes drafts of the questions presented and the conclusion headings for our analysis. Writing these now will help limit how often you need to refer back to the task documents. You can revise the issues and conclusion headings after you complete the analysis, but if you do happen to run out of time before revising, your answer will still show that you can write an issue and guide your reader with headings.

Thus, at this point, we can add another layer to our schematic with the two issues and key facts we've identified. Schematic Layer 2 shows the new information that we added after reading Kay's letter in blue text.

Schematic Layer 2. After Reading the File

To: Steve Ramirez
From: Examinee
Date: July 30, 2014
Re: Modification of Retainer Agreements

QUESTIONS PRESENTED

I. What does Kay need to do under the rules of professional conduct to ethically modify her retainer agreements with current clients to cover future fee disputes?

II. How, if at all, does Kay need to revise her proposed language to be legally enforceable?

BRIEF ANSWERS

I.

II.

FACTS

Our client, Kay Struckman, would like to add a provision to her existing clients' retainer agreements that requires arbitration of fee disputes. In exchange for clients agreeing to this new provision, Kay will forgo her annual fee increases for two years.

"Any claim or controversy arising out of, or relating to, Lawyer's representation of Client shall be settled by arbitration, and binding judgment on the arbitration award may be entered by any court having jurisdiction thereof."

ANALYSIS

I. What does Kay need to do under the rules of professional conduct to ethically modify her retainer agreements with current clients to cover future fee disputes?

II. How, if at all, does Kay need to revise her proposed language to be legally enforceable?

CONCLUSION

Notice that these headings are phrased as questions, not as conclusions. That's because we just copy-and-pasted them from our Questions Presented into the spots in the office memo where the conclusion headings will go.

This is fine! We will change them into conclusion headings once we know the answers to the questions. For now, they are useful reminders about what each issue is about and, if we run out of time, they will function as headings. If we have time, though, we should rewrite them as conclusion headings.

Other Things That Look Like Rules or Instructions That You Can't Easily Categorize

Ah but wait, there's more to the task memo that we haven't accounted for in our schematic:

- "Your memorandum should include support for your conclusions with citation to legal authority, taking care to distinguish contrary authority where appropriate."
- "Be sure to set forth those conditions in your memorandum."

These two sentences start with commands so you know that they are rules or instructions. But what are they telling you to do? And how do you account for them in your schematic?

The first instruction means that you should write conclusions and support them with citations to legal authority. In other words, use C-RAC structure and include legal citations. We were already planning to do so because we are writing an office memo, which uses C-RAC structure and legal citations. The last clause, cautioning you to "distinguish contrary authority where appropriate," means you should pay attention to authority that conflicts with the legal authorities that you are using to support your conclusion and write about that contrary authority, explaining why it is less applicable to your facts than the supporting authority. We should add that part to our schematic so we don't forget it.

This second instruction is a specific request to describe the conditions necessary to modify Kay's retainer agreements to require arbitration for fee disputes. The specificity of this request likely means that the graders will be looking for those conditions, so we'll want to make them easy to spot. Perhaps they could have their own headings in each issue's analysis. Or perhaps we could add a new section to our office memo. Either way, we should add this instruction to our schematic so we don't forget it.

Let's add a third layer to our schematic that accounts for these additional instructions. Schematic Layer 3 shows these parts, analysis structure information, and additional instructions; Layer 3 additions are in blue text.

After you've practiced writing a lot of schematics and MPTs, you might internalize some of these instructions, like "include legal citations." Once you no longer regularly refer to these instructions when writing your MPT answers, you can stop adding them to your schematic. You also might have added these instructions to the first layer of your schematic.

Schematic Layer 3. Incorporating Additional Analysis Structure

To: Steve Ramirez
From: Examinee
Date: July 30, 2014
Re: Modification of Retainer Agreements

QUESTIONS PRESENTED

I. What does Kay need to do under the rules of professional conduct to ethically modify her retainer agreements with current clients to cover future fee disputes?

II. How, if at all, does Kay need to revise her proposed language to be legally enforceable?

BRIEF ANSWERS

I.

II.

FACTS

Our client, Kay Struckman, would like to add a provision to her existing clients' retainer agreements that requires arbitration of fee disputes. In exchange for clients agreeing to this new provision, Kay will forgo her annual fee increases for two years.

"Any claim or controversy arising out of, or relating to, Lawyer's representation of Client shall be settled by arbitration, and binding judgment on the arbitration award may be entered by any court having jurisdiction thereof."

ANALYSIS

I. What does Kay need to do under the rules of professional conduct to ethically modify her retainer agreements with current clients to cover future fee disputes?
R — include contrary authority
A — distinguish contrary authority
C
List conditions necessary to ensure modification is ethical:

II. How, if at all, does Kay need to revise her proposed language to be legally enforceable?
R — include contrary authority
A — distinguish contrary authority
C
List conditions necessary to ensure modification is legally enforceable:

CONCLUSION

Outlining the Law

We've finished reading the task documents, which comprised the entire MPT file. We don't have any more facts to read. So now we'll turn to the library, which contains the relevant law.

◊ Hot Tip

> Sometimes the most efficient way to write an MPT is to read the library before reading factual documents in the file. This particular MPT has very few facts, so reading the whole file before beginning the library makes sense.

From the MPT's table of contents, we can see that Steve has given us five legal authorities:

1. The relevant rule of professional conduct from Franklin, Rule 1.8. This rule is from our jurisdiction, Franklin, and so is binding.
2. A state bar ethics opinion from the neighboring state of Columbia. This ethics opinion is not from our jurisdiction, Franklin, and so it is not binding. However, we learned in the task memo that Franklin and its neighboring states, Columbia and Olympia, all use the same Rule 1.8.
3. A 2006 case from the Franklin Court of Appeal, which is binding.
4. A 2004 case from the Franklin Court of Appeal, which is binding.
5. A 2009 case from the Olympia Supreme Court, which is not binding but is from a neighboring state's highest court.

From this table of contents, we can tell that there is a mix of binding and non-binding law. We'll want to flag non-binding law that we rely on for our analysis. Perhaps we'll get lucky and the contrary law that Steve warned us about will also be non-binding. That would make distinguishing contrary law simple.

At this point, we'll read the legal authorities and begin to outline the law in our schematic, so we'll only have to write it once, and we can easily move words and sentences around on the screen. Remember that you are reading the legal authorities so that you can use them to advise Kay. Look for legal tests and similar fact patterns that would make useful examples. Add them to your schematic as you read.

Schematic Layer 4 shows the completed schematic, with our notes on the law in blue text.

Schematic Layer 4. Analysis Structure

To: Steve Ramirez
From: Examinee
Date: July 30, 2014
Re: Modification of Retainer Agreements

QUESTIONS PRESENTED

I. What does Kay need to do under the rules of professional conduct to ethically modify her retainer agreements with current clients to cover future fee disputes?

II. How, if at all, does Kay need to revise her proposed language to be legally enforceable?

BRIEF ANSWERS

I.

II.

FACTS

Our client, Kay Struckman, is a sole practitioner who represents individuals and small businesses. She would like to add a provision to her existing clients' retainer agreements that requires arbitration of fee disputes. In exchange for clients agreeing to this new provision, Kay will forgo her annual fee increases for two years.

"Any claim or controversy arising out of, or relating to, Lawyer's representation of Client shall be settled by arbitration, and binding judgment on the arbitration award may be entered by any court having jurisdiction thereof."

ANALYSIS

I. What does Kay need to do under the rules of professional conduct to ethically modify her retainer agreements with current clients to cover future fee disputes?
R—include contrary authority
- Modifying a retainer agreement with an existing client is a business transaction under Rule 1.8. Comment to Franklin Rule of Professional Conduct 1.8.
- To enter into a business transaction with a client, Rule 1.8 requires the following: (1) the terms of the transaction must be fair, in writing, and written in a way that the client can reasonably understand, (2) the attorney must advise the client in writing that it's desirable for the client to seek independent legal advice about the transaction, and (3) the client must give informed consent, also in writing. Franklin Rule of Professional Conduct 1.8.
- Attorney cannot prospectively limit malpractice liability unless the client is independently represented in making the agreement. Franklin Rule of Professional Conduct 1.8.
- Concern about vulnerable clients not having the same understanding of the implications as a lawyer, particularly "those small business and individual clients who lack the benefit of in-

How do we know for sure that this authority ──────▶ should be italicized?

We don't. We just made a choice to italicize it. Our thinking was that an ethics opinion is more like a judicial opinion than a statute, so italics would be appropriate.

If we hadn't italicized it, that would also be okay. The MPT doesn't provide a citation rulebook to follow, so just use your best judgment and try to be consistent.

house counsel or other resources to advise them about arbitration." *Columbia Ethics Opinion*.

- "Where parties enter into an agreement openly and with complete information, arbitration represents an appropriate and even desirable approach to resolving such disputes." *Lawrence*. [*Lawrence* determines that agreement is legally unenforceable and so does not get to ethics question. Is this the right order?]

- Sloane summarizes the requirements of Rule 1.8 and describes a retainer agreement that clearly meets the standards "for any issue other than attorney malpractice." *Sloan v. Davis* (Olympia Sup. Ct. 2009). [analogy]

A—distinguish contrary authority

- Kay's clients are mostly small businesses and individuals, although some of them have asked for arbitration clauses in the contracts Kay drafts for them.

C

List conditions necessary to ensure modification is ethical:

II. How, if at all, does Kay need to revise her proposed language to be legally enforceable?

R—include contrary authority

- Courts enforce binding arbitration clauses in retainer agreements "only where the client has been explicitly made aware of the existence of the arbitration provision and its implications." *Lawrence v. Walker* (Fr. Ct. App. 2006).

- A binding arbitration clause "should be interpreted most strongly against the party who created the uncertainty." *Lawrence*.

- Attorney has the burden of proving she acted in good faith when agreeing to binding arbitration and that her client knowingly agreed to binding arbitration. *See Lawrence*.

- A legally enforceable agreement requiring binding arbitration must meet five conditions: (1) It must provide for a neutral arbitrator. (2) It must provide for more than minimal discovery. (3) It must require a written, reasoned decision. (4) It must provide for all of the types of relief that would be available if the disputing party went to court. And (5) it cannot require employees to pay unreasonable fees or costs as a condition of access to the arbitration forum. *Johnson v. LM Corp.* (Fr. Ct. App. 2004).

- Franklin Supreme Court requires "a written decision giving reasons for the decision" in any arbitration proceeding (citing *Lake v. Whiteside* (Fr. Sup. Ct. 1994)). This requirement does not need to be built into the arbitration agreement because it is assumed that arbitrators will follow the law and write a decision explaining their reasons. *Johnson*.

- Exorbitant arbitration agreement fees and costs frustrate the ability of the disputing party to pursue its claims. *Johnson.*
- Arbitration agreement must clearly describe what the fees and costs of the arbitration would be and how those expenses would be divided between the two parties. *Johnson.*

A — distinguish contrary authority

C

List conditions necessary to ensure modification is legally enforceable:

CONCLUSION

E. Sample Completed Task: Office Memo

Here is the sample completed office memo task that builds upon the schematic this chapter demonstrated.

One note about this particular sample: it is overly complete and far longer than any MPT answer that you would be able to write in ninety minutes on bar exam day. Because we walked you through the creation of this completed task in this chapter, we didn't want to leave out any of the material you saw earlier. However, you should *not* feel that your answers must be this long or complex to earn a strong score on the MPT. They do not.

Sample Completed Office Memo Task

To: Steve Ramirez
From: Examinee
Date: July 30, 2014
Re: Modification of Retainer Agreements

QUESTIONS PRESENTED

I. What does Kay need to do under the rules of professional conduct to ethically modify her retainer agreements with current clients to cover future fee disputes?

II. How, if at all, does Kay need to revise her proposed language to be legally enforceable?

BRIEF ANSWERS

I. Yes, Kay can probably ethically include a mandatory arbitration clause for fee disputes in her retainer agreements if she limits the clause to "fee disputes," explains the possible effects of the clause in plain language and in writing, and encourages her clients to get independent legal advice before signing the agreement.

II. Yes, Kay can include a legally enforceable mandatory arbitration clause for fee disputes in her retainer agreements if she revises and expands upon her proposed language.

We wrote these brief answers by copying the conclusion headings from our Analysis and pasting them here. We then added "Yes" to the beginning of each sentence because that's how brief answers usually begin.

On the MPT, copy-and-paste when you can. Doing so will save time.

FACTS

Our client, Kay Struckman, is a sole practitioner who represents individuals and small businesses. She would like to add a provision to her existing clients' retainer agreements that requires arbitration of fee disputes. In exchange for clients agreeing to this new provision, Kay will forgo her annual fee increases for two years. Kay has included agreements like this in some of her clients' contracts. Kay hasn't had any fee disputes, but if any arise, she wants them to be resolved quickly and with minimal costs for both Kay and her clients.

This is the provision she has drafted: "Any claim or controversy arising out of, or relating to, Lawyer's representation of Client shall be settled by arbitration, and binding judgment on the arbitration award may be entered by any court having jurisdiction thereof."

Kay would like to know what changes need to be made to ensure that the new arbitration provision is ethical and legally enforceable.

ANALYSIS

Between the last schematic layer and our final answer, we changed the questions to conclusion headings. This one is pretty detailed. The second one is less detailed. Sometimes you have time for a high level of detail in your conclusion headings, and sometimes you don't.

I. Kay can probably ethically include a mandatory arbitration clause for fee disputes in her retainer agreements if she limits the clause to "fee disputes," explains the possible effects of the clause in plain language and in writing, and encourages her clients to get independent legal advice before signing the agreement.

A lawyer who modifies a retainer agreement with an existing client is governed by Rule 1.8 of the Franklin Rules of Professional Conduct. *See* Comment to Franklin Rule of Professional Conduct 1.8 (explaining that modifying a retainer agreement with an existing client is a business transaction under Rule 1.8). To modify a retainer agreement with an existing client, Rule 1.8 requires the following:

(1) The terms of the transaction must be "fair and reasonable to the client," fully disclosed, and written "in a matter that can be reasonably understood by the client."

(2) The attorney must advise the client in writing that it is "desirable" for the client to seek independent legal advice about the transaction and give the client an opportunity to consult independent counsel.

(3) The client must give informed consent, also in writing, "to the essential terms of the transaction and the lawyer's role in the transaction, including whether the lawyer is representing the client in the transaction."

Franklin Rule of Professional Conduct 1.8. Rule 1.8 also prohibits lawyers from entering into agreements that prospectively limit their liability to clients for malpractice, unless the client is independently represented. Franklin Rule of Professional Conduct 1.8.

However, with respect to arbitration requirements, "where parties enter into an agreement openly and with complete information, arbitration represents an appropriate and even desirable approach to resolving such disputes." *Lawrence v. Walker* (Fr. Ct. App. 2006).

The neighboring state of Columbia has an identical Rule 1.8 and issued an ethics opinion stating that a lawyer cannot meet the requirements of Rule 1.8 by modifying a retainer agreement with an existing client to add an arbitration requirement for any future malpractice claim. *Columbia State Bar Ethics Committee Ethics Opinion 2011-91.* The *Columbia Ethics Opinion* questioned whether some clients could actually understand the benefits and drawbacks of arbitration compared with litigation. *Id.* The *Columbia Ethics Opinion* was particularly concerned about vulnerable clients not having the same understanding of the implications as a lawyer, specifically "those small business and individual clients who lack the benefit of in-house counsel or other resources to advise them about arbitration." *Id.* Moreover, lawyers' fiduciary duty to their clients implies a "heightened obligation" to be "fair and reasonable" that will make it "very difficult for lawyers to meet their obligations as fiduciaries." *Id.*

On the other hand, the high court of the neighboring state of Olympia described a retainer agreement that "provided that the parties would use binding arbitration to resolve *any disputes* concerning Davis's representation." *Sloane v. Davis* (Olympia Sup. Ct. 2009) (emphasis added). First, the arbitration process was fair, although not described in more detail than that. *Id.* The requirements for a fair arbitration process are listed in a Franklin Court of Appeal opinion and described in detail in the next section of this memo. *See Johnson v. LM Corporation* (Fr. Ct. App. 2004). Second, the disclosure was in writing and easily understandable to the client because she sent her client a copy of the retainer agreement and a brochure explaining arbitration. *Sloane.* The brochure described types of matters that might be arbitrated (including the claim at issue), examples of arbitration procedures that could differ from litigation procedures, and standards for arbitrators, including that they disclose conflicts of interest, follow the law, award remedies appropriately, and issue a written decision. *Id.* And third, the brochure explained that the client could and should get the advice of another attorney before signing the retainer agreement. *Id.* The *Sloane* opinion differed from the *Columbia Ethics Opinion* in a few ways, one being that the arbitration provision would not limit the court's ability to discipline attorneys who violate the norms of practice. *Id.; Columbia Ethics Opinion.* Another being that *Sloane* assumes that arbitrators will follow the law, including any legal limits on malpractice liability. *Sloane.*

Although neither the *Columbia Ethics Opinion* nor *Sloane* are binding in Franklin, they do suggest that Kay can ethically add the provision to her existing retainer agreements. To ensure that she is meeting her ethical obligations, she should tailor the language to just fee disputes, which would clearly exclude malpractice claims from the arbitration clause. Excluding malpractice claims would address the *Columbia Ethics Opinion*'s concern that limiting malpractice liability cannot be adequately explained to non-lawyer clients.

This paragraph contains practical suggestions for Kay. Although office memos do not always include practical suggestions for the partner or client, they seem appropriate here because Kay had requested advice about how to make sure her arbitration clauses meet the rules of professional conduct. This paragraph also allows us to incorporate some of the other facts that didn't have an obvious place in the preceding application paragraph.

She should also consider creating a brochure like the one described in *Sloane* because that brochure met Rule 1.8's requirements for modifying a retainer agreement with an existing client. Doing so would address the *Columbia Ethics Opinion*'s concern about small businesses and individuals, which are exactly who comprise the majority of Kay's clients. That Kay is willing to forgo two years of rate increases does make the agreement more fair and reasonable, so she should keep that aspect of her plan. Because Kay has already drafted arbitration clauses for some of her clients' contracts, she could adapt any explainers she has written for her clients about the effect of adding a mandatory arbitration clause to a contract.

II. Kay can include a legally enforceable mandatory arbitration clause for fee disputes in her retainer agreements if she revises and expands upon her proposed language.

Courts enforce binding arbitration clauses in retainer agreements "only where the client has been explicitly made aware of the existence of the arbitration provision and its implications." *Lawrence v. Walker* (Fr. Ct. App. 2006). The attorney has the burden of proving she acted in good faith when agreeing to binding arbitration and that her client knowingly agreed to binding arbitration. *See id.* A binding arbitration clause with uncertain language "should be interpreted most strongly against the party who created the uncertainty." *Id.* For example, a retainer agreement that requires arbitration for "disputes regarding legal fees and any other aspect of our attorney-client relationship" does not specify which kinds of claims are included in the "any other aspect" language. *Id.* The *Lawrence* court held that this uncertainty meant that, as a matter of contract, the attorney and client did not agree to mandatory binding arbitration of a malpractice claim, the claim at issue in *Lawrence. Id.*

A legally enforceable agreement requiring binding arbitration must meet five conditions:

(1) It must provide for a neutral arbitrator. *Johnson v. LM Corp.* (Fr. Ct. App. 2004).

(2) It must provide for more than minimal discovery. *Id.* However, even if the agreement limits discovery, for example by allowing only three depositions, the Franklin Court of Appeal assumed "that an arbitrator would permit additional discovery if a proper showing were made," just as in a court proceeding. *Id.* Although two years later, that

same court stated that "arbitrators, unlike judges, are not required to follow the law." *Id.*

(3) It must require a written, reasoned decision. *Id.* However, the Franklin Supreme Court requires "a written decision giving reasons for the decision" in any arbitration proceeding. *Id.* (citing *Lake v. Whiteside* (Fr. Sup. Ct. 1994)). This requirement does not need to be built into the arbitration agreement because it is assumed that arbitrators will follow the law and write a decision explaining their reasons. *Id.*

(4) It must provide for all the types of relief that would be available if the disputing party went to court. *Id.*

(5) It cannot require employees to pay unreasonable fees or costs as a condition of access to the arbitration forum. *Id.* Exorbitant arbitration agreement fees and costs frustrate the ability of the disputing party to pursue its claims. *Id.* Therefore, arbitration agreement must clearly describe what the fees and costs of the arbitration would be and how those expenses would be divided between the two parties. *Johnson.*

Some of these requirements overlap with the ethical requirements described in Section I of this analysis. For example, requirement 4 that the agreement provide for all the types of relief that would be available if the disputing party went to court requires the same information as Rule 1.8's requirement that the agreement be fair and reasonable and, "fully disclosed, and written in a matter that can be reasonably understood by the client." Rule 1.8.

Here, Kay should tailor her proposed language to narrow "any claim or controversy" to "fee disputes," to avoid creating an agreement that is unenforceable because it doesn't specify the types of disputes it applies to. She should also expand the proposed language to include the five conditions listed above, from *Johnson*. This might require additional research into arbitration fees and costs and how to fairly divide them between Kay and her client, should arbitration arise.

CONCLUSION

In conclusion, Kay can ethically include a legally enforceable mandatory arbitration clause for fee disputes in her retainer agreements if she revises and expands upon her proposed language in these ways:

To be consistent with our use of "*id.*" as a short form citation earlier in the document, this short cite should say "*id.*" rather than "*Johnson.*" The "*Johnson*" is left over from the schematic. We remembered to italicize the citation but not to change it to an "*id.*"

This is okay! We left this oversight here on purpose. Perfection is not the goal on the MPT, and some inconsistent citation formatting in your answer is not going to lower your MPT score.

We created this list by copying and pasting words we had already written in the analysis and formatting those words into this fancy-looking list.

(1) Tailor her proposed language to narrow "any claim or controversy" to "fee disputes."

(2) Expand the proposed language in the agreement to include these five items:

   a. Provide for a neutral arbitrator.

   b. Provide for more than minimal discovery.

   c. Require a written, reasoned decision.

   d. Provide for all the types of relief that would be available if the disputing party went to court.

   e. Clearly describe what the fees and costs of the arbitration would be and how those expenses would be divided between the two parties and ensure that those fees and costs are reasonable.

(3) Give her clients a brochure that describes

   a. the types of matters that might be arbitrated (fee disputes only);

   b. examples of arbitration procedures that could differ from litigation procedures, and standards for arbitrators, including that they disclose conflicts of interest, follow the law, award remedies appropriately, and issue a written decision; and

   c. that the client could and should get the advice of another attorney before signing the retainer agreement.

Chapter 5

MPT Core Genre: Brief

A brief is one of the three core genres that you must be able to write with confidence when you take the MPT. Here, we'll give you the basics of writing briefs to refresh your recollection. But if you have never written a brief, you might want to supplement this section with a first-year legal writing textbook.

In general, a brief is a document that a lawyer uses to convince a decision-maker (usually a judge) to make a decision in favor of her client. For example, a trial brief might be written to convince a trial judge to dismiss a case. Or an appellate brief might be written to convince a panel of appellate judges that the trial judge erred by dismissing the case. Although the audience for a brief is usually a judge, lawyers also write briefs for administrative hearing officers, regulatory bodies, and other non-judge decision makers. On the MPT, you might be asked to write a "brief" or "persuasive memorandum" for a non-judge decision maker. However, you will still be writing a brief.

Because the purpose of a brief is to convince a decisionmaker to rule in your favor, briefs are conclusion-to-analysis documents. Before you even start thinking about the facts or the law, you already know the conclusion of your analysis. If you're writing a brief, you start with the conclusion that your client wins. Then you figure out how to make the facts and the law fit together to convincingly (and ethically) support that conclusion.

A. Know Your Task

The MPT can ask you to write a brief (or variant thereof) in many different ways. The simplest is when the task memo asks you to write the argument section of a trial brief. That label will almost certainly be accurate, and you can proceed with creating the schematic for the argument section of a trial brief.

But sometimes the MPT will ask you to write a "persuasive memorandum" or just a "memorandum," and what the MPT is expecting is not an office memo but instead a document that reads like a brief, even if it has the overall look of an office memo. To determine whether a request for a "memorandum" is really a brief, you need to analyze the audience and purpose. (To review how to do an analysis of your task documents to figure out your task, review Chapter 3, How to Take the MPT.)

B. Annotated Description of a Typical Trial Brief

Here is an annotated description of a typical trial brief. Remember: it is very unlikely that you will be asked to write a full trial brief or appellate brief on the MPT. As of the printing of this book, no MPT has set that task for examinees. Instead, you'll most likely be asked to write only the argument section of the brief. Nevertheless, seeing an annotated description of a full brief will refresh your recollection of what briefs look like and provide some context for what's happening in the argument section.

Annotated Description of a Trial Brief

STATE OF FRANKLIN, EDWARD COUNTY SUPERIOR COURT

Yolany Trejo,   )
    Plaintiff,   )
    v.   )   No. 20-CVS-0513
Ernest Steigerwald,   )
    Defendant.   )

This part of a trial brief is called the caption. The caption includes the jurisdiction and court, the parties and their roles (e.g., plaintiff and defendant), and the docket or case number. It is highly unlikely that you will have to write a caption for an MPT brief.

DEFENDANT'S BRIEF IN SUPPORT OF HIS MOTION FOR
SUMMARY JUDGMENT ◄────────

Brief introduction that names the parties, briefly describes the legal issue(s), and asks for the particular relief that is desired, like to grant summary judgment in this example. ◄────

This is the title of the brief. It is highly unlikely that you will have to write a title for an MPT brief.

It is highly unlikely that you will have to write an introduction for an MPT brief. If you do, it can be short.

FACTUAL BACKGROUND ◄────

Describe the legally relevant facts but convey them using a structure and details that make your client's position look favorable and sets up your legal argument. Use paragraphs to divide the story into logical parts. Include the case's procedural history in this part of the brief or in its own "Procedural History" part, depending on local court rules or your boss's preferences.

It is unlikely that you will have to write the factual background section for an MPT brief. If you do, it can be short. (If the MPT asks you to write the factual background, the reason is probably because there are not very many facts to write about.)

ARGUMENT

The Argument part of your brief contains your legal analysis—the relevant law and how it applies to your facts to support the conclusion that you want the decisionmaker to reach. (Remember that briefs are conclusion-to-analysis documents.) The Argument is composed of C-RACs.

Funnel: The first passage contains rules that apply to the whole Argument section, organized from the most general to the most specific. We call this a "funnel" section. Not every Argument will have a funnel. Often the funnel in a trial brief will include the procedural standard—such as the rule of civil procedure that governs summary judgment and some additional information from case law. ◄────

Trial briefs usually ask a judge to make a decision on a matter of procedure—like granting summary judgment or excluding evidence—and thus trial briefs typically include a procedural passage that describes the relevant rules.

If the authorities in your MPT library include procedural rules, that is a sign that you should include procedural rules in your brief.

Roadmap: If your Analysis has a funnel, the last part of the funnel is a sentence that summarizes the major conclusions of your Argument. Not every Argument needs a roadmap.

Briefs on the MPT typically ——→ I. Conclusion Heading 1: Write a conclusion heading for each
have more than one issue.   issue. These headings should be complete sentences that
Or, if they have just one   state the conclusion of your analysis on that issue (the first
issue, then that issue has   C of your C-RAC). You might see this style of heading re-
clear sub-issues.   ferred to as a "point heading" or "argument heading." If
                                    your brief has only one big issue, then you should still
This example includes an   write a conclusion heading.
issue that contains two
sub-issues. You'll use sub-   Funnel (if necessary): This funnel should include the legal test that
headings like this if the legal applies to the first issue. In this example, the legal test has two
test that governs this issue elements: element A and element B. Include a short roadmap that
has two parts, such as two   previews the conclusions of the two elements.
elements, two factors, two
prongs, or two steps. Be on ——→ A. Subheading A: Write a conclusion heading for
the lookout for tests with   element A.
multiple parts. Unless your
quirky boss tells you   Rules: Write the rules that apply to the facts of your case,
otherwise, use those parts   including examples and rules that weaken your conclusion. Pres-
to create sub-headings and   ent the rules from most general to most specific, with examples
sub-sections, with each   typically last. Use legal citations. When possible, frame the rules
sub-section addressing one   in a way that helps you prove your desired conclusion.
part (e.g., element, factor,
prong, step).   Application: Apply the law from your "rules" section to the facts
                              of your case. If you wrote a rule example, compare the facts of
                              your case to the facts of the example case to either show how
On the MPT, use the ————   the cases are similar or how they are different, depending on
informal citation style the   which helps you prove your desired conclusion. Divide your ap-
MPT requires and we teach   plication into paragraphs as necessary. Address any weaknesses
in Chapter 3, "How to Take   in your conclusion, including contrary law, but try to make the
the MPT".   weaknesses work in your favor or minimize the weaknesses as
                              unimportant to drawing the conclusion.

                         B. Subheading B: Write a conclusion heading for
                             element B.

                   Rules: More rules here, like above.

                   Application: More application here, like above.

                    II. Conclusion Heading 2, if necessary

                   Rules: More rules here, like above.

                   Application: More application here, like above.

                              CONCLUSION

                   After the conclusion, many trial briefs include a certificate of serv-
                   ice and other procedural necessities. These items depend on court
                   rules. On the MPT, you will not be asked to reproduce a certificate
                   of service or any other of its kind.

C. Sample Schematic Layers

In this section, we will demonstrate how to write the layers of a sample schematic for the argument section of a trial brief.[1] As you read, imagine that you are watching a bar writer take an MPT. Each schematic layer will be introduced with the step that the writer was engaged in when that portion of the schematic was made. The bar writer is creating the schematic as she reads the MPT file and library, rather than waiting until she has finished reading all of the MPT materials.

Read the Task Memo and Guidelines

In a one-page task memo from our quirky boss, senior partner Rick, we learn the following:

- We are *defending* a client against a negligence lawsuit that has already been brought. This means that we are already in litigation.
- The plaintiff has made "three separate claims of injury due to negligence." This statement suggests that we will need to structure our document around these three claims. However, we don't yet know that Rick wants us to write a brief. For example, Rick might want an office memo to help him prepare for a negotiation.
- Procedurally, we've finished discovery and now want to move for summary judgment.
- Rick wants us to "prepare the argument section of our brief" to support the summary judgment motion. This is a clear indication that the genre is a brief, a trial brief more specifically. We are starting with the conclusion of "my client is not liable for the plaintiff's three claims of negligence."
- Rick has specifically instructed us to write only the argument section of the trial brief. This means that we should not include the other parts of a real-life trial brief, like the caption, introduction, facts, and conclusion. However, Rick does say to "incorporate relevant facts into your argument." We probably don't need to add this to our schematic, though, because Rick's request just means that we should use C-RAC to make the argument. (And we were going to do that anyway.)

---

1. The sample schematic and sample answer are both based on MPT-1 from July 2013.

- Rick warns us not to address comparative negligence or damages. This is good news because it limits the scope of our task.
- He also tells us that there are "guidelines for the preparation of persuasive briefs" that we should follow. We should look at these guidelines and incorporate them into our schematic, but more likely than not the guidelines won't tell us anything we haven't already learned (or know) about "persuasive briefs." (Note: These guidelines do not vary much from MPT to MPT, so if you've practiced several brief MPTs, it's unlikely that you will be surprised by the guidelines if you do get them on the real MPT.)

We can write layer 1 of our schematic right now. After practicing the techniques in this book, you should be able to begin writing your MPT answer as soon as you finish reading the task memo, which is typically only one page long.

Schematic Layer 1. Argument Section of a Brief

ARGUMENT

Funnel

I. Summary judgment should be granted to defendant on plaintiff's first claim of negligence. ◄──────

In general,

For example,

Here,

Thus, defendant is not liable to plaintiff for breaking her nose after running into a wall after being scared by a costumed character in the haunted house.

II. Summary judgment should be granted to defendant on plaintiff's second claim of negligence.

In general,

For example,

Here,

Thus, defendant is not liable to plaintiff for injuring her ankle after slipping on a muddy path in the mock graveyard behind the haunted house.

III. Summary judgment should be granted to defendant on plaintiff's third claim of negligence.

In general,

For example,

Here,

Thus, defendant is not liable to plaintiff for breaking her wrist on the way to the parking lot after being scared by a costumed character. ◄──────

By using "plaintiff" and "defendant" instead of the parties real names, we don't have to keep remembering the parties' names or type them out repeatedly. The graders will probably be relieved to see this shorthand as well.

Because we don't know yet the legal reason why our client is entitled to summary judgment, we'll just write very general conclusion headings at the start. If we have time to expand them later, we can. If not, we've got our headings written.

After writing this first heading, we can copy and paste the same heading into the other two sections and just change the word "first" to "second" and "third."

We can fill in the conclusions with a little more detail because we know which injury goes with which claim. Again, this is a pretty general conclusion that doesn't explain why defendant isn't liable. But at least we have a conclusion and we know what this issue is about.

Great! We've already written so much, including a basic structure for our argument. Let's move on to the next document, which describes the guidelines for trial briefs. In these guidelines we learn the following:

- Each argument should support our position by analyzing applicable law and arguing that the law and facts together support our position. This sounds like C-RAC, which was already our plan.
- Although we should emphasize supporting authority, we also need to cite and address contrary authority by explaining it or distinguishing it. Explaining away or distinguishing contrary authority is a key feature of conclusion-to-analysis documents, which was also already our plan.
- The guidelines warn us, with underlined language, not to write "exaggerated, unsupported arguments." This is really good advice for any legal document and hopefully advice that you've heard many times before.
- Next the guidelines give us some information about structure:
  - We should divide the argument into its major components. Helpfully, our schematic is already divided into the three issues that our boss identified for us.
  - Each major component should include a heading that is a complete sentence that "summarize[s] the arguments each covers." These headings sound like conclusion headings, and we already wrote drafts of them in our schematic.
- Finally, the guidelines say *not* to prepare a list of other document parts that are not the Argument section. We already knew that we should write *only* the Argument section, which forecloses the need to write any other sections.

Having reviewed the guidelines, what do we need to add to our schematic? Nothing. Layer one already accounts for everything in these guidelines.

Read the Law

For this example, we're going to start by reading the law first rather than reading the facts. For this particular MPT, this is a good choice, because the facts in this MPT's file are on the long side, eight pages. The library, on the other hand, contains only two cases and is five pages long. When you encounter an MPT with similar amounts of facts and law, consider reading the law first.

In Schematic Layer 2, new additions are indicated with blue text.

Schematic Layer 2. Argument Section of a Brief

ARGUMENT

Summary judgment should be granted when "there is no genuine dispute of material fact and the moving party is entitled to judgment as a matter of law." Larson v. Franklin High Boosters Club, Inc. (Fr. Sup. Ct. 2002). A "material fact" is one that would affect the outcome of the case. Id.

The threshold question in a negligence claim is whether the defendant owed a duty to "act reasonably under the circumstances and not put others in positions of risk." Larson. If the defendant does owe a duty, then the court needs to determine the scope of that duty by addressing these three things: (1) what duty the defendant owed given the particular circumstances, (2) whether the defendant breached that duty and caused an injury or loss, and (3) whether the risk that caused the injury "was encompassed within the scope of the protection extended by the imposition of that duty." Larson. Whether the plaintiff is actually aware of the risk is not part of the analysis. Larson. Instead, the test focuses on the defendant and whether it acted unreasonably with respect to the plaintiff. Larson.

The "particular circumstances" include the setting in which the injury occurred. Larson.
- Customers at an event that is designed to be scary attend with an expectation that they will be scared. Larson. Therefore, operators of scarily designed events have no duty to prevent customers from reacting in scared and unexpected ways because those reactions are exactly why customers attend scarily designed events like haunted houses. Larson.
- On Halloween particularly, customers of a haunted house should certainly expect to be scared and to react accordingly. Larson.

Businesses can owe an additional duty to customers that it invites onto its premises. Larson. Businesses owe an additional duty to protect their customers from "unreasonably dangerous conditions." Larson.
- An unreasonably dangerous condition is a danger that a reasonable person would expect to injure a "prudent person using ordinary care under the circumstances." Costello.
- An accident caused by a dangerous condition does not automatically mean that the condition is *unreasonably* dangerous. Costello v. Shadowland Amusements, Inc. (Fr. Sup. Ct. 2007) (citing Parker v. Muir (Fr. Sup. Ct. 2005)).

Early in the first case is a paragraph describing the summary judgment standard. That's the kind of motion we're making, so just copy that standard into your document when you see it.

Notice that this case name is not italicized. Why not? Because adding italics slows down some writers, and speed is of the essence when writing a schematic during an MPT. So those writers don't use italics in their schematics.

This is an okay thing to do! Ideally, you'll have enough time to italicize case names and other citation components when you're turning your schematic into a paragraphs. But if you don't, that is also okay! Having citations where you need them is far more important.

The middle of the first opinion uses the phrase "standard for liability," which suggests that a legal test is about to follow. And it describes "duty" as the starting point of a negligence analysis. If you've been studying torts, then you probably can quickly recall that the elements of negligence are duty, breach, causation, and injury. This opinion extends the duty question to include determining the duty's scope, then it combines breach, causation, and injury.

This looks like another big test beyond the duty one that we already wrote. We'll put those rules here until we have a better sense of how all the rules fit together with each other and our three issues.

Note the persuasive phrasing here. ——————→

- A dangerous condition is unreasonably dangerous only if the plaintiff can prove (1) that the owner knew or should have known about the dangerous condition, (2) the injury could have been prevented by the defendant exercising reasonable care, and (3) the defendant did not exercise reasonable care. Costello.
- To meet this additional duty, courts consider many factors. Costello.
   - Whether businesses have adequate physical facilities as well as sufficient employees who can supervise the customers. Larson. For example, in a haunted house, the business can meet this duty by training scary-costumed employees how to respond if a customer is injured. See Larson.
   - The business's history of accidents caused by the dangerous condition. Costello.
   - How well the customers can observe the dangerous condition. Costello.

A brief illustration here of getting startled by someone scary because we know from the task memo that being startled by a scary person is involved in issues #1 and #3.

In Larson, the plaintiff was startled by an employee dressed as a vampire who "came at him suddenly" in a haunted house, causing the plaintiff to trip over his feet and fall, injuring himself. Larson. The plaintiff won.

Although the law is generally outlined here, it's not yet distributed through the three sections we've prepared because we need to know the facts to divvy the law up properly.

In Parker, there was no unreasonably dangerous condition when a customer tripped over a rock on a path through a cornfield maze. Parker. A reasonable person would expect rocks to be on a dirt path and would not injure herself on them. Parker. In addition, this was the first injury to occur in the corn maze. Parker.

I. Summary judgment should be granted to defendant on plaintiff's first claim of negligence.
In general,
For example,
Here,
Thus, defendant is not liable to plaintiff for breaking her nose after running into a wall after being scared by a costumed character in the haunted house.

II. Summary judgment should be granted to defendant on plaintiff's second claim of negligence.
In general,
For example,
Here,
Thus, defendant is not liable to plaintiff for injuring her ankle after slipping on a muddy path in the mock graveyard behind the haunted house.

III. Summary judgment should be granted to defendant on plaintiff's third claim of negligence.

In general,

For example,

Here,

Thus, defendant is not liable to plaintiff for breaking her wrist on the way to the parking lot after being scared by a costumed character.

Read the Facts

For Schematic Layer 3, we have new information from the facts, indicated with blue text. You'll also notice that we've redistributed the rule examples to the issues that seem to match. We left the rest of the law in place and focused on distributing the legally relevant facts into the three sections of the Argument. Another way to create this layer of the schematic would be to distribute more of the law among the funnel and three issues. We chose not to because it wasn't immediately clear where some of the rules should go, given the overlap among some of the issues—particularly 1 and 3, which share the fact of a costumed employee scaring the plaintiff, who then hurts herself.

Schematic Layer 3. Argument Section of a Trial Brief

ARGUMENT

Summary judgment should be granted when "there is no genuine dispute of material fact and the moving party is entitled to judgment as a matter of law." Larson v. Franklin High Boosters Club, Inc. (Fr. Sup. Ct. 2002). A "material fact" is one that would affect the outcome of the case. Id.

The threshold question in a negligence claim is whether the defendant owed a duty to "act reasonably under the circumstances and not put others in positions of risk." Larson. If the defendant does owe a duty, then the court needs to determine the scope of that duty by addressing these three things: (1) what duty the defendant owed given the particular circumstances, (2) whether the defendant breached that duty and caused an injury or loss, and (3) whether the risk that caused the injury "was encompassed within the scope of the protection extended by the imposition of that duty." Larson. Whether the plaintiff is actually aware of the risk is not part of the analysis. Larson. Instead, the test focuses on the defendant and whether it acted unreasonably with respect to the plaintiff. Larson.

The "particular circumstances" include the setting in which the injury occurred. Larson.

- Customers at an event that is designed to be scary attend with an expectation that they will be scared. Larson. Therefore, operators of scarily designed events have no duty to prevent customers from reacting in scared and unexpected ways because those reactions are exactly why customers attend scarily designed events like haunted houses. Larson.

- On Halloween particularly, customers of a haunted house should certainly expect to be scared and to react accordingly. Larson.

Businesses can owe an additional duty to customers that it invites onto its premises. Larson. Businesses owe an additional duty to protect their customers from "unreasonably dangerous conditions." Larson.

- An unreasonably dangerous condition is a danger that a reasonable person would expect to injure a "prudent person using ordinary care under the circumstances." Costello.

- An accident caused by a dangerous condition does not automatically mean that the condition is *unreasonably* dangerous. Costello v. Shadowland Amusements, Inc. (Fr. Sup. Ct. 2007) (citing Parker v. Muir (Fr. Sup. Ct. 2005)).

- A dangerous condition is unreasonably dangerous only if the plaintiff can prove (1) that the owner knew or should have known about the dangerous condition, (2) the injury could have been prevented by the defendant exercising reasonable care, and (3) the defendant did not exercise reasonable care. Costello.

- To meet this additional duty, courts consider many factors. Costello.
    - Whether businesses have adequate physical facilities as well as sufficient employees who can supervise the customers. Larson. For example, in a haunted house, the business can meet this duty by training scary-costumed employees how to respond if a customer is injured. See Larson.

- The business's history of accidents caused by the dangerous condition. Costello.
- How well the customers can observe the dangerous condition. Costello.

For safety, defendant stations individuals around the haunted house, including at least one in each room, to help customers if needed. The zombie in the last room was there for the dual purpose of scaring and helping customers, as was the masked chainsaw man outside the fence. All employees, including those two, were told to offer help to customers and to call the doctor in the event of a medical emergency. A doctor is at the park at all times.

Defendant employs a doctor at the park when the park is open.

I. Summary judgment should be granted to defendant on plaintiff's first claim of negligence.

In general,

For example,

In Larson, the plaintiff was startled by an employee dressed as a vampire who "came at him suddenly" in a haunted house, causing the plaintiff to trip over his feet and fall, injuring himself. Larson. The plaintiff won.

Here,

Because plaintiff thought it would be fun to be frightened and scared, she and her husband went to the Haunted House attraction on Halloween evening, which was the first night that the attraction was open. She and her husband walked through several rooms that had spooky stuff in them, which scared her enough to let out small screams. When they arrived in the last room of the house, it was lit by only a few dim lightbulbs and a light-up "exit" sign. Then a woman dressed as a zombie jumped out of a hiding place and yelled loudly. Plaintiff was so scared that she shrieked and attempted to run away from the zombie and instead ran face-first into a wall, breaking her nose.

Zombie person kept coming towards her after she ran into the wall. Plaintiff did not ask the zombie person for help, noticed that the zombie person was talking to her but could not understand the zombie person over her crying.

Neither plaintiff nor husband asked for help.

Defendant instructed the zombie not to touch customers, to ensure that people were having good Halloween fun, and to help customers who need it, including by calling a doctor if the customer has a medical emergency. The zombie did offer to help plaintiff, but plaintiff did not hear her.

Zombie was 17 but had basic first aid training.

Thus, defendant is not liable to plaintiff for breaking her nose after running into a wall after being scared by a costumed character in the haunted house.

II. Summary judgment should be granted to defendant on plaintiff's second claim of negligence.

In general,

For example,

In Parker, there was no unreasonably dangerous condition when a customer tripped over a rock on a path through a cornfield maze. Parker. A reasonable person would expect rocks to be on a dirt path and would not injure herself on them. Parker. In addition, this was the first injury to occur in the corn maze. Parker.

Here,

When plaintiff left the haunted house, she was walking on a pathway through a mock graveyard. The pathway was illuminated by small lights. She could see that the ground was "really muddy," and she knew that the last three days had been very rainy. She slipped and fell in the mud, twisting her ankle.

Nobody else was in the mock graveyard. Plaintiff did not ask for help. The graveyard was enclosed by the same fence that enclosed the haunted house, so a reasonable customer would have known that the attraction had not ended when she exited the house.

Thus, defendant is not liable to plaintiff for injuring her ankle after slipping on a muddy path in the mock graveyard behind the haunted house.

III. Summary judgment should be granted to defendant on plaintiff's third claim of negligence.

In general,

For example,

Here,

After plaintiff left the mock graveyard but while she was still on the amusement park's grounds, a man wearing a hockey mask and holding what plaintiff thought was a chain saw, jumped out from behind a fence that plaintiff and her husband were approaching. Startled, plaintiff fell again and she broke her wrist. Her husband yelled at the chain saw man, who backed off.

This area was lit by lampposts and plaintiff could see well.

Thus, defendant is not liable to plaintiff for breaking her wrist on the way to the parking lot after being scared by a costumed character.

D. Sample Completed Task:
Argument Section of a Trial Brief

Here is the sample completed argument section of a trial brief task that builds upon the schematic this chapter demonstrated.

Please note that our sample answers aren't perfect models that cover every substantive point, nor are they beautifully written. Instead, they reflect what we believe most examinees can write within 90 minutes, if they prepare well for the MPT. If you look at the point sheets for the sample answers, you'll see they are longer and address more substantive points than most of our samples. If you have looked at sample answers from bar prep companies, you'll notice that their sample answers are longer than ours. It's the rare examinee who will be able to write such comprehensive answers in 90 minutes. Moreover, such lengthy responses are not necessary to do well on the MPT. Indeed, if your response is lengthy because it meanders and lacks focus, a grader may have trouble understanding it.

Sample Completed Argument Section of a Trial Brief Task

ARGUMENT

Summary judgment should be granted when "there is no genuine dispute of material fact and the moving party is entitled to judgment as a matter of law." *Larson v. Franklin High Boosters Club, Inc.* (Fr. Sup. Ct. 2002). A "material fact" is one that would affect the outcome of the case. *Id.* Here, no material facts are disputed and defendant is entitled to judgment as a matter of law.

The threshold question in a negligence claim is whether the defendant owed a duty to "act reasonably under the circumstances and not put others in positions of risk." *Id.* If the defendant does owe a duty, then the court needs to determine the scope of that duty by addressing these three things: (1) what duty the defendant owed given the particular circumstances, (2) whether the defendant breached that duty and caused an injury or loss, and (3) whether the risk that caused the injury "was encompassed within the scope of the protection extended by the imposition of that duty." *Id.* Whether the plaintiff is actually aware of the risk is not part of the analysis. *Id.* Instead, the test focuses on the defendant and whether it acted unreasonably with respect to the plaintiff. *Id.*

Businesses owe an additional duty to protect their customers from "unreasonably dangerous conditions." *Id.* An unreasonably dangerous condition is a danger that a reasonable person would expect to injure a "prudent person using ordinary care under the circumstances." *Costello v. Shadowland Amusements, Inc.* (Fr. Sup. Ct. 2007) (citing *Parker v. Muir* (Fr. Sup. Ct. 2005)). An accident caused by a dangerous condition does not automatically mean that the condition is *unreasonably* dangerous. *Id.* (citing *Parker v. Muir* (Fr. Sup. Ct. 2005)).

Here, because plaintiff was an invitee of defendant, a business, defendant did owe plaintiff a duty to protect its customers from unreasonably dangerous conditions. However, as to all three of plaintiff's claims, defendant met its duty and is therefore entitled to summary judgment.

I. Summary judgment should be granted to defendant on plaintiff's first claim of negligence because defendant trained its employees to help plaintiffs, including by calling a doctor in the event of a medical emergency, and therefore met its duty to protect its customers from unreasonably dangerous conditions.

In general, to prove that a business breached its duty to protect customers from unreasonably dangerous conditions, the plaintiff must show (1) that the business knew or should have known about the dangerous condition, (2) the injury could have been prevented by the business exercising reasonable care, and (3) the business did not exercise reasonable care. *Costello.* Many factors should be considered when determining whether a defendant did not exercise reasonable care. *Id.*

One factor is the setting in which the injury occurred. *Larson.* Customers at an event that is designed to be scary, like a haunted house, attend with an expectation that they will be scared. *Larson.* Therefore, operators of scarily designed events have no duty to prevent customers from reacting in scared and unexpected ways because those reactions are exactly why customers attend scarily designed events like haunted houses. *Id.* On Halloween particularly, customers of a haunted house should certainly expect to be scared and to react accordingly. *Id.*

Another factor is whether businesses have adequate physical facilities as well as sufficient employees who can supervise the customers. *Id.* For example, in a haunted house, the business can meet this duty by training scary-costumed employees how to respond if a customer is injured. *See id.* Two additional factors are the business's history of accidents caused by the dangerous condition and how well the customers can observe the dangerous condition. *Costello.*

For example, in *Larson*, the plaintiff was startled by an employee dressed as a vampire who "came at him suddenly" in a haunted house, causing the plaintiff to trip over his feet and fall, injuring himself. *Larson.* The Supreme Court of Franklin could not determine whether the defendant had met its duty because the record did not include information about the employees and their training. *Id.*

Here, on the other hand, defendant has presented evidence that it met its duty to exercise reasonable care for its customers. First, as in *Larson*, the mere fact that a scarily dressed employee jumped in front of a customer was itself not an unreasonably dangerous condition.

Second, unlike in *Larson*, the record shows that defendant took customer safety seriously. It stationed employees around the haunted house, including at least one in each room, to help customers if needed. The zombie who scared plaintiff in the last room was there for the dual purpose of entertaining customers by scaring them and helping customers if they needed it. All employees, including the zombie, were told to offer help to customers and to call the doctor in the event of a medical emergency. Defendant ensures that a doctor is at the park all the time. Indeed, defendant instructed the zombie not to touch customers, to ensure that people were having good Halloween fun, and to help customers who need it, including by calling a doctor if the customer has a medical emergency. The zombie, who had basic first aid training, did offer to help plaintiff, but plaintiff did not hear her. Nor did plaintiff or her husband ask for help.

Third, plaintiff was the only person to be injured at the haunted house. And fourth, plaintiff could see that she was in a haunted house filled with scary things because she had gone to the attraction for just that purpose and she and her husband walked through several rooms that had spooky stuff in them, which scared her enough to let out small screams. All of these factors weigh in defendant's favor.

Thus, defendant is not liable to plaintiff for breaking her nose after running into a wall after being scared by a costumed character in the haunted house.

II. Summary judgment should be granted to defendant on plaintiff's second claim of negligence because the muddy path that plaintiff slipped on was not an unreasonably dangerous condition.

In general, dangerous conditions are not unreasonably dangerous if the customer can see the dangerous condition and would reasonably expect that the condition could cause injury if not approached cautiously. *See Parker.*

For example, in *Parker*, there was no unreasonably dangerous condition when a customer tripped over a rock on a path through a cornfield maze. *Id*. A reasonable person would expect rocks to be on a dirt path and would not injure herself on them. *Id*.

Here, plaintiff could see the dangerous condition of the muddy pathway and a reasonable person would expect that a muddy pathway should be approached cautiously. The path that plaintiff slipped and fell on was a pathway through a mock graveyard. The pathway was illuminated by small lights. She could see that the ground was "really muddy," and she knew that the last three days had been very rainy. Moreover, the graveyard was enclosed by the same fence as enclosed the haunted house, so a reasonable customer would have known that the attraction had not ended when she exited the house.

Thus, defendant is not liable to plaintiff for injuring her ankle after slipping on a muddy path in the mock graveyard behind the haunted house.

III. Summary judgment should be granted to defendant on plaintiff's third claim of negligence.

Running low on time? Just leave the placeholder headings from your schematic in place. They're not perfect, but they do the job of telling your reader where the third issue gets argued.

As described in more detail in Section I of this brief, the mere fact that a scarily dressed employee jumped in front of a customer was itself not an unreasonably dangerous condition. See Larson.

Sometimes you don't have time to properly format your citations. That's okay. Having them where you need them is far more important than putting them in italics or using appropriate short forms.

Here, all of the same factors applied to plaintiff's first claim apply here. First, the chainsaw man had received the same instructions as other employees, including the zombie: scare the customers to entertain them and offer help if they need it, including by calling a doctor in the event of a medical emergency. Defendant had a trained employee exactly where it might have needed one — where customers might be scared and act so strangely that they hurt themselves. Second, although plaintiff could not see the chainsaw man until he jumped out from behind the fence, the area was well lit by lampposts. Moreover, she was still on the amusement park's grounds and reasonably should have expected that more scary entertainment might occur. Indeed, she was barely out of the haunted house attraction when the fright occurred.

Thus, defendant is not liable to plaintiff for breaking her wrist on the way to the parking lot after being scared by a costumed character.

Chapter 6

MPT Core Genre: Letter

A letter is one of the three genres that you must be able to write with confidence when you take the MPT. Here, we'll give you the basics of writing letters to refresh your recollection. But if you have never written a letter, you might need to supplement this section with a legal writing textbook that covers letters (client letters or demand letters are most common).

In general, a letter is a document that a lawyer uses to communicate formally, and in writing, with another person or persons. Letters come in many variants, including client letters, decision letters, demand letters, and opinion letters. Each variant has a distinct purpose, so a letter *generally* is a form for accomplishing that purpose through formal, written, interpersonal communication.

Like office memos and briefs, letters have standard parts. But unlike office memos and briefs, letters can have many audiences and many purposes. Letters can be written to other lawyers on your team, opposing counsel, clients, potential clients, judges, administrative boards, and so on. And the purpose might be to convince your audience of a particular conclusion or to explain why the analysis leads to a particular conclusion. In other words, a letter can be a conclusion-to-analysis document or an analysis-to-conclusion document.

A. Know Your Task

When the MPT asks you to write a letter, the task memo will use the word "letter." At that point, you know that your answer should look like a letter and contain the parts of a letter.

The type of letter depends on what the rest of the task documents say. For example, a demand letter will always be a conclusion-to-analysis document. But a client letter or opinion letter could be an analysis-to-conclusion document or a conclusion-to-analysis document. Look for phrases like "to persuade" or "to convince." Words of persuasion usually indicate that your boss has told you the desired outcome in advance, and you now need to come up with an argument to support that desired outcome.

On the other hand, if you see phrases like "to predict" or "to analyze whether," then your letter is an analysis-to-conclusion document. Your boss and your client might have a preferred outcome, but your task is to give a balanced analysis so that they can make sound decisions. (To review how to do an analysis of your task documents to figure out your task, review Chapter 3, How to Take the MPT.)

B. Annotated Description of a Typical Letter

Here is an annotated description of a typical letter. If you are asked to write a letter, you can start with this basic format. As you'll see, the most important part of the letter is the body of the letter. The **body of the letter** is where most of your legal analysis goes and also where you'll need to make judgments about how to present this analysis.

If your letter is an analysis-to-conclusion document, then the body of the letter will probably resemble the analysis part of an office memo. If your letter is a conclusion-to-analysis document, then the body of the letter will probably resemble the argument part of a brief. Just as you exercise judgment about how to structure those parts of an office memo and a brief, you'll need to exercise judgment about how to structure the body of a letter.

Annotated Description of a Letter

The sender's name
And address should
Go here or be centered
At the top, like letterhead.

The date goes here, in this format: month day, year

Recipient's name
Recipient's firm or organization
First line of recipient's address
Second line of recipient's address

Greeting:

Paragraph 1: Introduce yourself. If you are writing on behalf of a client, say that you represent the client. If appropriate, include a pleasantry. Then tell the recipient the purpose of your letter, preferably in one or two sentences. And end the paragraph with a conclusion related to that purpose. For example, tell your client the most likely outcome of her legal claim or tell opposing counsel what you want their client to do for yours.

Paragraph 2: Briefly describe the relevant factual background to ensure that you and the recipient know the same things about the issue that you are writing about. ◄

Body of the Letter: The body of the letter contains your legal analysis. It serves the same function as the analysis section of an office memo or the argument section of a brief. C-RAC is still an appropriate way to convey your analysis, and conclusion headings can still be helpful signposts for readers if you are addressing multiple issues or sub-issues. However, in letters, it can also be more appropriate to introduce law in the application section. Citations are another flexible convention. You will definitely use formal legal citations in a letter if your boss tells you to. You might also use formal legal citations if your recipient has legal training and will know how to read them.

Last Paragraph: In this paragraph, you should restate your conclusion from the first paragraph and describe any next steps that the recipient should take, including a deadline if appropriate.

Sign-off,

Supervisor's name
Supervisor's title

The default greeting is "Dear" followed by an honorific (like Ms. or Dr.) and the recipient's last name. If you aren't sure whether to address the letter to a Mr. or a Ms., use the recipient's full name. If you know that the recipient prefers to be addressed as Mrs. or Mx., then use the recipient's preferred honorific. (Mx. is a gender-neutral honorific.)

A pleasantry could be "I hope you are doing well." Or "I'm following up on our recent phone call."

Sometimes task memos will explicitly ask for this factual background, and sometimes task memos will explicitly ask you to omit this factual background. Do whatever your quirky boss says to do. If your quirky boss says nothing, then write a few sentences of factual background.

The default sign-off is "Sincerely," but there are other common lawyer-y variations like "Sincerely yours" or "Respectfully."

C. Sample Schematic Layers

In this section, we will demonstrate how to write the layers of a sample schematic for a demand letter.[1] As you read, imagine that you are watching a bar writer take an MPT. Each schematic layer will be introduced with the step that the writer was engaged in when that portion of the schematic was made. The bar writer is creating the schematic as she reads the MPT file and library, rather than waiting until she has finished reading all of the MPT materials.

Read the Task Memo

In a one-page task memo from our quirky boss, senior partner Henry, we learn that Henry wants us to write a letter for Henry's signature. This means that Henry will be signing and sending the letter after he reviews it. The task memo includes an overview of our client's situation—she is in trouble at work for taking unapproved leave—and some instructions for the letter.

First, Henry has told us that the letter will be sent to the top human resources executive at our client's employer. We don't know whether this executive is a lawyer or a non-lawyer, but he is likely familiar with the FMLA, so he is probably an expert at this area of the law. We should avoid legal jargon that is not about the FMLA, though.

Second, Henry has told us that we will argue that our client is entitled to the leave she took. Thus we know the conclusion we're arguing for, and this is a conclusion-to-analysis document.

Third, Henry gives us some guidance about the letter. He's provided guidelines for demand letters, and we should follow those guidelines. If we weren't sure what kind of letter we were writing before, we definitely know now. He says to include a persuasive legal argument, to cite legal authorities, and to respond to the arguments that the employer has already raised. Even though our audience might not be a lawyer, our quirky boss wants us to include legal citations.

After practicing the techniques in this book, you should be able to begin writing your MPT schematic as soon as you finish reading the task memo, which is typically only one page long. Schematic Layer 1 shows a schematic created using what we learned from the task memo.

---

1. The sample schematic and sample answer are both based on MPT-2 from July 2014.

Schematic Layer 1. Demand Letter

Burton and Fines LLC
Attorneys at Law
963 N. Oak Street
Swansea, Franklin 33594

The sender's address came from the letterhead at the top of our task memo from Henry.

July 28, 2020

Mr. Steven Glenn
Vice President of Human Resources for Signs, Inc.
[address]

We don't know Mr. Glenn's address, but we know it will need to be added later. One way to handle this is to write a placeholder like this one, which shows where the address will eventually go.

Dear Mr. Glenn:

I represent Linda Duram, a graphic artist employed by Signs, Inc. Your company recently denied Ms. Duram's request for FMLA leave, placed Ms. Duram on probation for allegedly leaving work without approved leave, and threatened to terminate her if she takes unapproved leave again. I write to ask you to reverse your decision denying Ms. Duram FMLA leave and to retract the termination threat.

I have enclosed the relevant medical records and an affidavit by Ms. Duram describing her relationship with her grandmother.

Sincerely,

Henry Fines

Great! Let's move on to the next document, which describes the guidelines for demand letters.

Demand Letter Guidelines

The guidelines don't add much new information. They describe the audience and purpose of a demand letter, emphasizing that the demand letter is advocacy and should persuade the audience to resolve the legal issue in our client's favor. They describe five items that need to be included in a demand letter, including a short description of the situation and a specific settlement claim. The other items are already in our schematic. The guidelines also warn us not to write in an "insulting" tone and not to misrepresent the law or facts. This is universally good advice when writing legal documents. Schematic Layer 2 shows the new information from the guidelines in blue.

Schematic Layer 2. Demand Letter

Burton and Fines LLC
Attorneys at Law
963 N. Oak Street
Swansea, Franklin 33594

July 28, 2020

Mr. Steven Glenn
Vice President of Human Resources for Signs, Inc.
[address]

Dear Mr. Glenn:

I represent Linda Duram, a graphic artist employed by Signs, Inc. Your company recently denied Ms. Duram's request for FMLA leave, placed Ms. Duram on probation for allegedly leaving work without approved leave, and threatened to terminate her if she takes unapproved leave again. I write to ask you to reverse your decision denying Ms. Duram FMLA leave and to retract the termination threat.

Short description of the facts

Thorough analysis of basis for claim

Responses to arguments raised against the claim

I have enclosed the relevant medical records and an affidavit by Ms. Duram describing her relationship with her grandmother.

End with specific settlement claim

Sincerely,

Henry Fines

Read the Facts

For this example, we're going to start by reading the facts. That could be a good choice here because the facts in this MPT are on the short side, about four pages. The library, on the other hand, is eight pages long and contains two statutes, five regulations, and two circuit court cases. That's a lot of law to read without knowing the client's case. New additions to Schematic Layer 3 are indicated with blue text.

Schematic Layer 3. Demand Letter

Burton and Fines LLC
Attorneys at Law
963 N. Oak Street
Swansea, Franklin 33594

July 28, 2020

Mr. Steven Glenn
Vice President of Human Resources for Signs, Inc.
[address]

Dear Mr. Glenn:

My name is Henry Fines, and I represent Linda Duram, a graphic artist employed by Signs, Inc. Your company recently denied Ms. Duram's request for FMLA leave, placed Ms. Duram on probation for allegedly leaving work without approved leave, and threatened to terminate her if she takes unapproved leave again. I write to ask you to reverse your decision denying Ms. Duram FMLA leave and to retract the termination threat.

Earlier this month, the morning after learning of her great-aunt's death, Ms. Duram emailed you to ask for five days of leave under the FMLA so that she could care for her grandmother while traveling to and attending Ms. Duram's great-aunt's funeral. As Ms. Duram told you in her email request, her grandmother was dying of heart disease and could not travel by herself. She needed a companion to administer medications and medical therapy and was understandably distraught when her sister died. As Ms. Duram also explained in her email, she was raised by her grandmother.

> This paragraph is the short description of the situation. We can add more to it if we learn that more facts are important once we read the law.

Later that day, you denied Ms. Duram's request for FMLA leave and gave four reasons that the FMLA did not cover Ms. Duram's request for leave. Each of these four reasons is legally incorrect, as the rest of this letter will explain.

> This paragraph finishes up the situation and introduces our four arguments. Our four arguments correspond to the four reasons that the employer gave for denying our client's leave request.

1. The FMLA does apply to caring for grandparents.

2. The FMLA does apply to travel.

3. The FMLA does apply to funerals.

4. Ms. Duram gave sufficient notice.

> We went ahead and turned those into conclusion headings by removing the "not" from the employer's statements. So where the employer said that the FMLA does not apply to funerals, we removed the "not" to state the opposite conclusion—the one we want for our client.

I have enclosed the relevant medical records and an affidavit by Ms. Duram describing her relationship with her grandmother.

End with specific settlement claim

Sincerely,

Henry Fines

After reading the facts, we know the four issues that we'll want to look for in the legal authorities, and we can read the eight pages of legal authorities with those issues in mind.

Read the Law

As we read the law, we can look for rules or examples that fit with our four issues and type those rules into the schematic. If we're thinking about the corresponding facts, we could type those in as well. New additions to Schematic Layer 4 are indicated with blue text.

Schematic Layer 4. Demand Letter

Burton and Fines LLC
Attorneys at Law
963 N. Oak Street
Swansea, Franklin 33594

July 28, 2020

Mr. Steven Glenn
Vice President of Human Resources for Signs, Inc.
[address]

Dear Mr. Glenn:

My name is Henry Fines, and I represent Linda Duram, a graphic artist employed by Signs, Inc. Your company recently denied Ms. Duram's request for FMLA leave, placed Ms. Duram on probation for allegedly leaving work without approved leave, and threatened to terminate her if she takes unapproved leave again. I write to ask you to reverse your decision denying Ms. Duram FMLA leave and to retract the termination threat.

Earlier this month, less than 24 hours after learning of her great-aunt's death, Ms. Duram emailed you to ask for five days of leave under the FMLA so that she could care for her grandmother while traveling to and attending Ms. Duram's great-aunt's funeral. As Ms. Duram told you in her email request, her grandmother was dying of heart disease and could not travel by herself. She needed a companion to administer medications and medical therapy and was understandably distraught when her sister died. As Ms. Duram also explained in her email, she was raised by her grand-mother.

Later that day, you denied Ms. Duram's request for FMLA leave and gave four reasons that the FMLA did not cover Ms. Duram's request for leave. Each of these four reasons is legally incorrect, as the rest of this letter will explain.

1.   The FMLA does apply to caring for grandparents.

Under the FMLA, eligible employees are entitled to twelve weeks of leave each year "[i]n order to care for the … parent … of the employee, if such … parent has a serious health condition. 29 U.S.C. ss 2612(a)(1)(C); see also 29 C.F.R. ss 825.12 (requiring em-

Here, we've used "ss" instead of the section symbol. Section symbols can be cumbersome to add when typing in test-taking software. If you find that's the case with your test-taking software, then type "ss" first. If you have time to go back and convert those to section symbols later, great! If not, the reader will know what you mean.

ployers to grant FMLA leave to care for a parent with a serious health condition).

- Under the FMLA, the term "parent" includes individuals who "stood in loco parentis" to the employee. 29 U.S.C. ss 2611(7).

- The FMLA does not define the term of "in loco parentis," which is usually defined by state law and in fact has been defined in the State of Franklin. Carson v. House Manufacturing, Inc. (15th Cir. 2013). In Franklin, "in loco parentis" applies to a person who purposefully and actually puts herself "in the situation of a lawful parent by assuming the obligations" of a parental relationship but without going through formalities such as adoption or guardianship. Id. To determine whether a person stood in loco parentis for a child, courts look at factors including the child's age and degree of dependence, as well as the amount of support that the person provided for the child. Id.

- For example, a grandfatjer was held to be acting in loco parentis to his grandson even though the child's parents never relinquished parentla rights and the grandfather never adopted the child. Carson (discussing Phillips v. Franlin City Park District (Fr. Ct. App. 2006)). In that case, the child lived in the grandfather's home from the age of four on, and the grandfather assumed the parental obligations of enrolling the child in school, taking the child to the doctor, providing day-to-day financial support, attending parent-teacher conferences at school, and volunteering for the child's Boy Scout troop. Id.

> There are typos in this schematic. That is a-okay. Typographic perfection is less important than quickly getting the law you need into your document. You'll be able to fix typos during the process of turning your schematic into a demand letter.

2. The FMLA does apply to travel.

- "Serious health condition" includes any illness that involves "continuing treatment by a health care provider." 29 U.S.C. ss 2611(11).

- "Continuing treatment" includes "a course of prescription medication … or therapy requiring special equipment to resolve or alleviate the health condition (e.g., oxygen)." 29 C.F.R. ss 825.113(c).

- Chronic conditions regulation. Necessary? ◄————

> This library included a lot of regulations, and it wasn't clear as we were reading that we needed this one about chronic conditions. So we flagged it and will come back to it later.

- For an employee "to care for" a parent with a serious health condition requires (1) that the employee "be in close and continuing proximity" to the parent and (2) that the employee offer "actual care" to the parent. Shaw v. BG Enterprises (15th Cir. 2011). If the employee is asking for leave to give psychological care for a parent with a serioius health condition, the parent must be receiving treatment for a physical or psychological illness. Shaw.

There's no law under this heading because we didn't see anything that was obviously relevant. Hopefully we'll figure something out as we write.

3.   The FMLA does apply to funerals.

4.   Ms. Duram gave sufficient notice.

When leave is not foreseeable, an employee must give her employer notice "as soon as practicable under the facts and circumstances of the particular case." 29 C.F.R. ss 825-303(a). The notice must include enough information "for an employer to reasonably determine whether the FMLA may apply to the leave request." 29 C.F.R. ss 825.303(b). [examples given, but look at case law first]

This regulation gives examples, which might be helpful as illustrations for analogies or distinctions. But at the time we read the regulations, we hadn't yet read any of the cases. And perhaps the cases will have better illustrations. We'll revisit this later as well.

Thorough analysis of basis for claim
Responses to arguments raised against the claim

I have enclosed the relevant medical records and an affidavit by Ms. Duram describing her relationship with her grandmother.

End with specific settlement claim

Sincerely,

Henry Fines

D. Sample Completed Task: Demand Letter

Here is the sample completed argument section of a demand letter task that builds upon the schematic this chapter demonstrated.

Please note that our sample answers aren't perfect models that cover every substantive point, nor are they beautifully written. Instead, they reflect what we believe most examinees can write within 90 minutes, if they prepare well for the MPT. If you look at the point sheets for the sample answers, you'll see they are longer and address more substantive points than most of our samples. If you have looked at sample answers from bar prep companies, you'll notice that their sample answers are longer than ours. It's the rare examinee who will be able to write such comprehensive answers in 90 minutes. Moreover, such lengthy responses are not necessary to do well on the MPT. Indeed, if your response is lengthy because it meanders and lacks focus, a grader may have trouble understanding it.

Sample Completed Demand Letter Task

While turning our schematic into paragraphs, we decided to center this address and make it look like letterhead. That is one formatting option for letters, if your exam software allows it.

Burton and Fines LLC
Attorneys at Law
963 N. Oak Street
Swansea, Franklin 33594

July 25, 2020

Mr. Steven Glenn
Vice President of Human Resources for Signs, Inc.
[address]

This is a placeholder to let the grader know that we understanding how to format a letter.

Dear Mr. Glenn:

My name is Henry Fines, and I represent Linda Duram, a graphic artist employed by Signs, Inc. Your company recently denied Ms. Duram's request for FMLA leave, placed Ms. Duram on probation for allegedly leaving work without approved leave, and threatened to terminate her if she takes unapproved leave again. I write to ask you to reverse your decision denying Ms. Duram FMLA leave and to retract the termination threat.

I have enclosed the relevant medical records and an affidavit by Ms. Duram describing her relationship with her grandmother, but here is a summary of the situation:

Earlier this month, less than 24 hours after learning of her great-aunt's death, Ms. Duram emailed you to ask for five days of leave under the FMLA so that she could care for her grandmother while traveling to and attending Ms. Duram's great-aunt's funeral. As Ms. Duram told you in her email request, her grandmother was dying of heart disease and could not travel by herself. She needed a companion to administer medications and medical therapy and was understandably distraught when her sister died. As Ms. Duram also explained in her email, she was raised by her grandmother.

Later that day, you denied Ms. Duram's request for FMLA leave and gave four reasons that the FMLA did not cover Ms. Duram's request for leave. As explained in more detail below, each of these four reasons is legally incorrect, and Ms. Duram was entitled to FMLA leave at the time she asked for it.

1.   The FMLA does apply to caring for grandparents.

Under the FMLA, eligible employees are entitled to twelve weeks of leave each year "[i]n order to care for the … parent … of the employee, if such … parent has a serious health condition. 29 U.S.C. ss 2612(a)(1)(C); *see also* 29 C.F.R. ss 825.12 (requiring employers to grant FMLA leave to care for a parent with a serious health condition).

Under the FMLA, the term "parent" includes individuals who "stood in loco parentis" to the employee, not just biological parents. 29 U.S.C. ss 2611(7). Although the FMLA does not define the term "in loco parentis," which is usually defined by state law, the term has been defined in the State of Franklin. *Carson v. House Manufacturing, Inc.* (15th Cir. 2013). In Franklin, "in loco parentis" applies to a person who purposefully and actually puts herself "in the situation of a lawful parent by assuming the obligations" of a parental relationship but without going through formalities such as adoption or guardianship. *Id.* To determine whether a person stood in loco parentis for a child, courts look at factors including the child's age and degree of dependence, as well as the amount of support that the person provided for the child. *Id.*

For example, a grandfather was held to be acting in loco parentis to his grandson even though the child's parents never relinquished parental rights and the grandfather never adopted the child. *Carson* (discussing *Phillips v. Franklin City Park District* (Fr. Ct. App. 2006)). In that case, the child lived in the grandfather's home from the age of four on, and the grandfather assumed the parental obligations of enrolling the child in school, taking the child to the doctor, providing day-to-day financial support, attending parent-teacher conferences at school, and volunteering for the child's Boy Scout troop. *Id.*

Here, like the grandmother in *Phillips*, Ms. Duram's grandmother was acting in loco parentis to Ms. Duram when Ms. Duram was a child. Like the child in *Phillips*, Ms. Duram's grandmother cared for Ms. Duram, fed her, clothed her, and took her to school and medical appointments for years. Even when Ms. Duram's parents were also living with her grandmother, it was her grandmother who fed her and ensured she kept up with school, attended extracurricular performances, and paid for summer camps.

We ran out of time and didn't go back and try to fix these shorthand "section symbol" abbreviations by replacing them with section symbols. This is okay! We spent the time on other aspects of the letter that we thought were more important.

Here, we combined headings 2 and 3 into a single heading (and section). We made this choice because we didn't find any law that applied only to funerals and not also to travel. The same law seemed to apply to both, and we were running low on time. Thus, for efficiency, we put the two issues together.

Does this violate our earlier instructions to use whatever analysis structure your quirky boss gives you (and cause graders to think you didn't answer the question properly)? It does, technically, because the boss gave us four arguments to address. But it's also an okay answer to write because, if you can't figure out how to write your boss's desired structure in the time allotted, you need to make a different choice that allows you to finish the task professionally—thus earning the highest possible grade.

Although Ms. Duram did not live solely with her grandparents as long as the child in *Phillips* did, she did live solely with her grandparents for at least four years before the end of high school. This is distinguishable from the child/employee in *Carson*, who spent "some weekends and extended vacations" with his grandparent during the last few years of high school. *See Carson.* In *Carson,* the primary caretaker was the child/employee's brother, with whom he primarily lived. *Id.*

Because Ms. Duram's grandmother acted in loco parentis to Ms. Duram, she qualifies as a "parent" under the FMLA and is thus covered by the act.

2. The FMLA does apply to travel, including traveling to funerals.

For an employee "to care for" a parent with a serious health condition requires (1) that the employee "be in close and continuing proximity" to the parent and (2) that the employee offer "actual care" to the parent. *Shaw v. BG Enterprises* (15th Cir. 2011). If the employee is asking for leave to give psychological care for a parent with a serious health condition, the parent must be receiving treatment for a physical or psychological illness. *Id.*

A "serious health condition" includes any illness that involves "continuing treatment by a health care provider." 29 U.S.C. ss 2611(11). "Continuing treatment" includes "a course of prescription medication ... or therapy requiring special equipment to resolve or alleviate the health condition (e.g., oxygen)." 29 C.F.R. ss 825.113(c).

Here, Ms. Duram's grandmother had a serious health condition, and Ms. Duram "cared for" her both before and during their travel to the funeral. Ms. Duram's serious health condition—end-stage congestive heart failure—was detailed by her doctor in the enclosed letter

This phrase tells the reader where this information came from—a letter from Ms. Duram's doctor. In general, the MPT does not expect you to cite to factual documents. Sometimes, as here, in your prose you want to describe the source of the information. That is an okay thing to do.

dated July 24. This congestive heart failure involved continuing treatment of administering oxygen, operating a heart pump, giving medications, and giving personal care that includes using a wheelchair for transportation. Ms. Duram's grandmother could not care for herself, including walking, bathing, and taking medications.

Ms. Duram learned how to perform all of these care tasks and cared for her grandmother for two months, with the help of a Home Health Service, before traveling to the funeral. She solely performed all of those care tasks, which required her to be in close and continuing proximity with her grandmother for the full five days of the requested leave time.

As for whether the FMLA applies to funerals, the FMLA does not explicitly exclude funerals. And it does apply to giving psychological care, which is what Ms. Duram was providing in addition to physical care.

3. Ms. Duram gave sufficient notice of her need for FMLA leave.

When FMLA leave is not foreseeable, an employee must give her employer notice "as soon as practicable under the facts and circumstances of the particular case." 29 C.F.R. ss 825-303(a). The notice must include enough information "for an employer to reasonably determine whether the FMLA may apply to the leave request." 29 C.F.R. ss 825.303(b). This information can include a condition that makes the employee unable to perform her job or a family member who is "under the continuing care of a health care provider." *Id.*

Here, Ms. Duram's notice was sufficient. First, her leave was not foreseeable, and she gave notice as soon as practicable. Her great-aunt's death was not planned or scheduled. Ms. Duram gave her employer notice at 9:15 a.m. the very next day after she learned of the death.

Second, the content of her notice was sufficient for Signs, Inc., to "reasonably determine whether the FMLA *may apply* to the leave request." See 29 C.F.R. ss 825.303(b) (emphasis added). Ms. Duram did not have to prove that the FMLA applied to her leave request; she only needed to give your company sufficient information that the FMLA could possibly apply. She did so in her July 7 email, which stated that her grandmother raised her and thus could be a "parent" under the FMLA; that her grandmother had heart disease and just a few months to live, a serious medical illness that required continuous care; that her grandmother could not care for herself, was depressed, and needed "medications and therapies."

Given Ms. Duram's strong legal position, I ask that you reverse your decision denying her FMLA leave and to retract the termination threat. Please respond in writing by August 5.

Sincerely,

Henry Fines

Chapter 7

The MEE Bar Essays

The purpose of this chapter is to familiarize you with the Multistate Essay Exam (MEE), which is the essay portion of the Uniform Bar Exam (UBE), and to give you test-taking techniques for writing them.

When looking at writing that you've done in the past, the MEE is most similar to the essay exams you likely wrote in law school. This chapter will teach you how to use your prior knowledge about writing law school exams and legal analysis generally to write the MEE and similar bar exam essays.

A. What Is the MEE?

If you are in a Uniform Bar Exam (UBE) jurisdiction, the MEE you will take is composed of six 30-minute essay questions. You will have three hours to complete these six essays, and you will be responsible for your time. If you are in a non-UBE jurisdiction, your exam may be composed of some or all of the MEE essay questions or similar bar essay questions.

Each year, the NCBE creates nine essay questions covering different subject areas. The UBE then assigns six of those essays to the UBE jurisdictions. Non-UBE jurisdictions can select which of the nine—or all nine—essays to assign.

The NCBE designs the MEE to test the examinee's ability to do the following in writing:

(1) **Spot the issues** buried in the facts.
(2) **Identify facts relevant** to your analysis.
(3) **Write a strong legal analysis** of the issues.

(4) **Know the law** to apply to your facts in order to write your analysis.[1]

You have written this kind of legal analysis many times before, on your law school exams and in your legal writing courses. Your law school exams are most similar to the MEE. **Both are legal analysis essays that use C-RAC structure.** Furthermore, like on the MEE, when you wrote your law school exams you did not have legal authorities at your disposal.

The point is, you already know how to write the genre the MEE is asking you to write. Every time you wrote your law school essay exams, you wrote the essay exam genre. It is a familiar genre to you.

What is unfamiliar to you is the MEE itself. Let's make the MEE familiar.

B. What You Are Writing

Law school essay exams and bar essays are of the same genre: legal analysis essays that use C-RAC structure. You approach them in similar ways: you receive a fact pattern, you use your knowledge of the law to identify issues in that fact pattern, and you analyze those issues by applying the law to the facts in writing using C-RAC structure.

You can also read Appendix 1, Legal Writing under Pressure, to review C-RAC structure and its important parts, such as conclusion headings.

You will use your knowledge of law school essay exams and C-RAC structure to create your schematics for your MEE answers.

♦ Hot Tip

Some sample MEE answers that you will see use IRAC analysis instead of C-RAC analysis. IRAC analysis begins with an issue, rather than with a conclusion. Unfortunately, with IRAC, the reader doesn't know the outcome of the analysis until she reads the end of the answer. We recommend using C-RAC as both a **test-taking strategy** and as **a legal-writing strategy** because C-RAC analysis is easier to read—and easier to grade—because you give the conclusion first.

---

1. The NCBE identifies the four skills like this: "identify legal issues raised by a hypothetical factual situation"; "separate material which is relevant from that which is not"; "present a reasoned analysis of the relevant issues in a clear, concise, and well-organized composition"; and "demonstrate an understanding of the fundamental legal principles relevant to the probable solution of the issues raised by the factual situation." National Conference of Bar Examiners, *The Multistate Essay Exam*, NCBEX.org.

C. Write the MEE

Each MEE question is one page, single-spaced. (Some run over onto two pages, but only a little, and that is rare.) At the top of the question is a fact pattern, and, usually, at the bottom are the prompts you must answer in your essay. Most MEE questions provide a short list of prompts (each with a single issue) to guide your answer. Some, however, give you one prompt, and you must break it into separate issues yourself.

MEE essays are unlike law school essay exams because, on law school exams, the fact patterns tend to be many pages long and the prompts are broadly worded so that you must spot all of the issues that you can. In many ways, then, the MEE essays are easier than your law school essay exams. This is great news! They're short, the prompts are precise, and there are only a few issues to spot. Also, they're designed to be completed in the time allowed.

If you are in a UBE jurisdiction, you will write six MEE essays in three hours, meaning each essay should take 30 minutes to write. Because you only have 30 minutes to write your answer, be sure you have a plan for how to apportion your time. If you can, set aside a few minutes at the end to write strong conclusions and check for any gaps in your rules or analysis.

If you have a strategy that worked well for your law school exams, you should use that strategy to write your MEE answers. However, if you would like some ideas for how to write your MEE essays, here are some tips to try on your practice MEEs. Remember: Do not try anything new on test day. Practice all of your test-taking strategies in advance.

Step 1. Read and Type the Prompts

When you start a new MEE essay, **read the prompts before reading the fact pattern**. Reading the prompts first helps you target which facts are relevant to the legal analysis.

After you read the prompts, type them into your exam software, numbered properly. These numbered prompts are the beginning of your schematic for your essay answer.

Step 2. Read the Facts and Add to Your Schematic

Go to the beginning of the fact pattern and read the facts all the way through one time. The facts are relatively short, as we mentioned, and having a full picture of the facts will help you identify which facts are important and which facts are not.

Now, go back and read the facts a second time. This time, as you read, look for facts that seem pertinent to the prompts you typed into your exam software. Type those pertinent facts under each prompt. If you type too many facts, that's okay; you can delete them later. Write them in a list, not in a paragraph. Remember that some facts might be pertinent to more than one prompt.

As you type the facts, type any legal rules that apply to the facts that you listed. You are brainstorming right now, and it is okay to be wrong. What is important is to get out all of the ideas you can as soon as you can think of them, especially laws that might apply to the facts you are reading.

Once you have finished reading the facts a second time, your schematic should contain the following:

- The specific MEE prompts for that essay.
- Under each prompt, a list of all of the relevant facts from the fact pattern paired with any applicable legal concepts you can think of.

Step 3. Write the Rule

Each MEE prompt that you typed into your schematic will eventually become a conclusion heading. You should write your conclusion headings last, though, after you figure out the answers to your prompts. Beneath each conclusion heading, write a complete C-RAC. To write a C-RAC, you need to start with a rule. (Review how to write conclusion headings in Appendix 1, Legal Writing under Pressure.)

Writing rules on the MEE is different than with professional legal genres because you do not have access to legal authorities. Because you do not have access to authorities, the rule passage of your MEE essay's C-RAC will likely be shorter than what you might write in an office memo. The only law that you have to generate your MEE rule passage is the black letter law that you've memorized. Also, you are not expected to write citations in MEE answers, although you can refer to foundational cases by name if you can recall them. (You might see citations in MEE sample answers from NCBEX or from bar prep companies, but they're just for show.)

Look at your first numbered prompt and at the facts and law you have listed beneath it. If you know the complete rule passage that applies to the prompt, great. Write that rule passage now. It is likely, though, that you won't be able to write a complete rule passage immediately. That's okay. If you know some of the rule, write what you know, from broadest to narrowest. (Review how to "funnel" a rule in Appendix 1, Legal Writing under Pressure.)

One of the main challenges of the MEE is that you are responsible for remembering the law and creating a rule passage from memory. But what if you can only recall bits and pieces of the law, or none at all?

Problem: You Recall Only Some of the Law

If you recall some of the law, write what you know in the rule passage of your schematic, and then move on to your application. You will likely recall more law as you apply law to your facts, and you can backfill the law as you go.

If you do not recall more law after writing your application, use your common sense to make up rules to fill in gaps, and apply the law that you have invented to the facts just as you would do if you were certain about the law. Don't give up on your structure just because there are holes in your legal knowledge. For example, if you remember two of the elements of a three-element test, you write a three-part analysis anyway, using common sense to create that third element for analysis.

Problem: You Recall None of the Law

If you can't recall the law at all, you have a different problem. To solve this problem, you should write to jog your memory. First, zoom out and identify the general area of law that the question is situated in. Torts? Criminal law? Contracts? Write that down.

Second, start listing any sub-areas of law that come to mind. Literally anything. Start typing those sub-areas into your exam software. Like this:

Torts: battery, negligence, products liability, *Palsgraf*, intentional infliction of emotional distress, invasion of privacy, defamation.

Writing this list might seem like a waste of time, but you aren't doing anything better by just staring at your blank screen. And, by listing all of the things that you do know, you will jog your memory. Your memory will (hopefully) draw connections between the facts of your fact pattern and the law that you know.

For example: You might type *Palsgraf* because you can't remember the phrase "proximate cause," but then you think of "causation" and negligence, and then you notice that the fact pattern has a backyard swimming pool and a near-drowning of a child. And *then* you remember the legal term *attractive nuisance*, which is the legal issue of your facts. Excellent! Your list brought you to the legal issue of your exam's fact pattern. Now you can delete your brainstorm and start writing. The entire process took you two minutes, and it was definitely not a waste of time.

If writing about the law to jog your memory doesn't work, return to the facts. As you read through the facts, ask yourself why each of the facts might have been included. If you think of a legal reason that a fact might be included—even if you can't think of a particular rule—type that legal reason into your schematic. Do the numbers not add up? (Think contracts.) Does anything seem unfair? (Think equity, or duty in negligence.) Often, reviewing the facts will help spark some recall about the law.

Sometimes, all you can do is use your gut to come up with what you think is the right answer, and then invent a rule that gets you to that right answer. Then write that rule with confidence, apply that rule with confidence, and move on.

Step 4. Write the Application

Although your rule passage might be on the short side, your application passage probably will not be. Apply the law to your facts as completely as you can. MEE essays lend themselves to detailed application passages, so be methodical about using the facts from your fact pattern. A good rule of thumb is that every sentence of application should contain a fact you can point to in the fact pattern and a phrase from a rule that you wrote in your rule passage. In other words, every fact should be paired with a rule.

When you start your application passage, start a new paragraph. Then, indicate that you are transitioning from your law passage by using the transition word "Here" at the beginning of your first application paragraph.

After you write your application passage, return to your rule passage and update it with any rules you might have remembered while applying the law.

Step 5. Write the Conclusions

Once you know your answer, rewrite your numbered prompts as conclusion headings. See Appendix 1, Legal Writing under Pressure, for help writing conclusion headings. For all bar writing (MPT or MEE), you need to be able to write conclusion headings swiftly.

Finally, for each numbered section, write a separate, final paragraph that begins, "In conclusion," and write your conclusion there. In most cases, you can simply paste your conclusion heading into your conclusion paragraph.

D. Practice the MEE

Now, you need to familiarize yourself with the MEE. Although you are more familiar with the process of writing exam essays because you wrote them in law school, you still need to practice the MEE. The more you practice, the more you will avoid surprises on test day. Familiarity is your friend.

When you practice an MEE, practice under test conditions. Use the focus mode in Microsoft Word or similar function in the writing software of your choosing. Use a pen or pencil to annotate your test packet as you will have limited access to writing implements on test day. Use a timing device to time yourself and be strict about time. Time pressure is a major factor on the bar exam, and so it should be a major factor in your bar practice. To practice MEEs, download past exams from NCBEX.org. You can also find practice MEEs in bar prep company materials.

After you write your practice MEE, you should evaluate it to help you improve. In Chapter 8, Evaluate Your Practice Tests, we show you how to evaluate your practice MEE answers.

E. Sample Answer

The sample answer we provide below is an answer to the Real Property question from the July 2013 MEE. You should download the MEE from that date, take that MEE, and compare your answer to this one. This sample answer we provide is not intended to be perfect. It is meant to be a good, but realistic, answer.

Notice the structure: each of the three prompts is numbered and then analyzed with an easy-to-follow C-RAC, beginning with a conclusion heading that applies law to the facts to reach a legal conclusion. The conclusion heading is in bold text so that it will be easy for the grader to see. If your exam software does not include a bolding option, use different formatting to make your conclusion heading stand out. For example, you could underline or even just put a space below the conclusion, as in the sample below.

After the conclusion heading, there is a rule passage (usually one paragraph). After the rule passage comes the application, with a transition indicated by the word "Here." The final paragraph of each section is a conclusion paragraph that begins with the phrase, "In conclusion." These transition words and phrases are essential to helping you write quickly and to cueing your reader as she grades your essay.

Sample MEE Real Property Answer[2]

1. No, the man is unlikely to prevail against the builder to recover the $80,000 he spent to repair the concrete because he is not in privity with the builder.

The sale of new construction carries an implied warranty that the new house is designed and constructed in a reasonably workmanlike manner and suitable for human habitation. In about half of jurisdictions, an implied warranty of habitability extends only to the original buyer of a home. In the other half, courts have extended the implied warranty past the original buyer on the theory that the builder has put a defective home into the marketplace. The deed by which a property's title is transferred is not relevant to the transfer of an implied warranty of habitability. A warranty deed, general or special, includes covenants relating to title, but not to the quality of the construction. Similarly, a quitclaim deed has to do with title: it releases whatever title interest the seller has in the property.

Here, the builder's implied warranty would cover the defective materials used to construct the man's home. If the man were the original owner of the home, he would have a claim against the builder. However, the man is the second owner of the home, and therefore he is not in privity with the builder. In about half of the jurisdictions, then, the builder's implied warranty does not extend to the man because of lack of privity. In those jurisdictions, the builder is not liable for the $80,000 that the man spent repairing the house because of defective materials that the builder used.

However, the defect arose only a little over a year after the home was in the marketplace. In some jurisdictions, the builder's implied warranty extends to the man, the home's second owner, on the theory that the builder put a defective home into the marketplace. If so, then the man can recover the $80,000 spent to repair the damage on the grounds of the implied warranty of habitability. The quitclaim deed under which he acquired the home is irrelevant because the quitclaim deed only has to do with title warranties, not with warranties of habitability.

In conclusion, the man is unlikely to prevail against the builder to recover the $80,000 he spent to repair the concrete because he is not in privity with the builder. However, if a jurisdiction extends the implied warranty to the man, then the man can recover.

---

2. This sample answer refers to the Real Property question on the July 2013 Multistate Essay Exam. You can download it from NCBEX.org.

2. No, the man is likely not personally liable for the outstanding balance on the mortgage note between the woman and the bank.

A mortgage that is not discharged when land is transferred stays with the land. A buyer can assume a mortgage by express agreement. If the buyer does not expressly assume the mortgage, then the buyer is not usually personally liable for the mortgage. However, if a buyer takes actions that imply assumption of a mortgage, then the buyer might be held liable under a theory of implied assumption. Furthermore, if the bank that holds the note forecloses on the mortgage, the buyer loses its interest in the property.

Here, the woman sold her property to the man by quitclaim deed that did not mention the mortgage, and the mortgage was not recorded. Furthermore, the man did not expressly assume the mortgage. By these facts alone, the man is not personally liable for the outstanding balance on the mortgage note between the woman and the bank.

However, the rest of the facts suggest that the man might be held personally liable under a theory of implied assumption. First, the sale by quitclaim deed was for $160,000 when the home was valued at $360,000 and the mortgage owed was $195,000. The difference between the home value and the price paid by the man was the value of the mortgage. Furthermore, he began paying the mortgage immediately after the purchase. These facts suggest the man intended to assume the mortgage and that the woman relied on him to do so.

In conclusion, the man is likely not personally liable for the outstanding balance on the mortgage note between the woman and the bank. However, if a court finds an implied assumption of the mortgage, then the man will be personally liable for the outstanding balance on the mortgage note.

3. No, the man will not be able to recover damages from the woman if the bank is successful in its foreclosure action because a quitclaim deed disclaims all warranties of title, including liens and mortgages.

A quitclaim deed, unlike a warranty deed, disclaims all warranties of title, including liens and mortgages. The grantee of a quitclaim deed may not sue the grantor of the deed for title defects.

Here, if the bank is successful in foreclosing on the man's property, he will not be able to recover any damages from the woman because she transferred the property to him via quitclaim deed. The quitclaim deed disclaimed all warranties of title, including mortgages, releasing the woman from liability for any title defects the property had. Therefore, the man cannot sue her for title defects, including the unpaid mortgage.

In conclusion, the man will not be able to recover damages from the woman if the bank is successful in its foreclosure action because a quitclaim deed disclaims all warranties of title, including mortgages.

Chapter 8

Evaluate Your Practice Tests

The purpose of this chapter is to help you learn from the practice MPTs and MEEs that you take. You will learn how to assess your performance on a practice exam and to identify areas for improvement.

Some of the strategies that you already use when revising and editing your legal writing are strategies you can use when evaluating your practice tests.

Our first suggestion for evaluating your practice tests is that you do it for each practice test you take—and that you carry forward what you learned from that evaluation. We recognize that evaluating a test you just took is hard work, sometimes just as hard as taking the test itself.

Our second suggestion is that you form a study group—even if that study group is composed of only you and one other person. You need to have someone else read your writing, and you need to have someone else's writing that you can read. Research shows that doing the work of peer feedback— both giving and receiving—is valuable to improving your work.[1]

With these two suggestions in mind—carrying forward what you learned and forming a study group—here are some strategies that you can use to evaluate your practice tests, including how to effectively use the grading materials from the NCBE and materials provided by bar prep companies.

---

1. *See generally* Cassandra Hill, *Peer Editing: A Comprehensive Pedagogical Approach to Maximize Assessment Opportunities, Integrate Collaborative Learning, and Achieve Desired Outcomes*, 11 Nevada Law Journal 667 (2011).

A. Reverse Outline

A **reverse outline** is an outline you create after you have finished writing a document. Reverse outlines help you better see what you wrote and where you put each thing you wrote.[2]

Reverse Outlines and the MPT

After you finish your practice MPT, do a reverse outline of your answer. To reverse outline a practice MPT, write a description of your document in the margins. You can either print your MPT and write in the margins with a pen, or you can use the comment-bubble feature of your writing software to write in the margins.

For example, to reverse outline a letter, you might first write "letterhead" and "greeting" in the margin where those features appear. For a document that uses C-RAC analysis, use the C-RAC annotations from Figure 8.1 (or shortened versions) in the margins.

Figure 8.1. C-RAC Annotations

- Conclusion
- Funnel
- Roadmap
- Procedural rule
- Rules
- Examples (a.k.a. rule or case illustrations)
- Rule synthesis
- Application (generally)
- Comparison
- Distinction
- Counterargument

After you write your reverse outline, look it over. Does anything look out of place? Or do you notice any parts or features that are missing?

---

2. For more on reverse outlining, see Rachel Gurvich and Beth Wilensky, "Add Reverse Outlining to Your Writing Toolbox," Sept. 5, 2017, *Before the Bar Blog*, American Bar Association, https://abaforlawstudents.com/2017/09/05/add-reverse-outlining-to-your-writing-toolbox/.

A common mistake when writing C-RAC legal analysis is to alternate between describing the law and applying the law to your facts. Instead, your legal analysis should describe all of the relevant law and then apply that law to your facts. If your reverse outline reveals that your legal analysis bounces between law and application, improve your work going forward. On your next practice MPT, keep rules together before applying them to your facts.

Another common mistake is describing an example from a case and failing to apply it to your facts, either as a comparison (analogy) or a distinction. You'll notice this on a reverse outline if you see an example from a case in the "R" section but no comparison or distinction in the "A" section. If you go through the trouble of describing an example from a case on the MPT, you should write a few sentences about how the facts in that example are similar to or different from the facts of your case.

Reverse Outlines and the MEE

Your practice MEE should contain one C-RAC for each issue you addressed. To evaluate your answer, including how well you followed the C-RAC structure, do a reverse outline with the same C-RAC annotations from Figure 8.1.

First look at each rule passage using the annotations from Figure 8.1. You might find that your rule passages are shorter than the rule passages in a typical legal analysis, but that's to be expected because you wrote your C-RACs without the help of legal authorities.

Now look to each application passage. Did you start your application passage with a new paragraph, and did you start that paragraph with the word "Here" signaling the transition to application? Did you apply law to all of the pertinent facts of your case? Does every sentence of your application passage contain both law and facts?

Did you set off your conclusion as a separate paragraph, and did you start that paragraph with the words "In conclusion" to signal for your reader the transition to conclusion?

B. Self-Evaluate

Often the reason we evaluate our own writing is because we need to revise it. Not so with bar writing. When you take the MPT and MEE, you will likely not have time to revise your completed answers during the test period. Instead, the reason to evaluate your practice MPTs and MEEs is so that you can improve the next MPTs and MEEs that you write.

Evaluating your practice bar writing goes beyond checking your answers against "answer keys" like the MPT point sheets or MEE sample answers. Checking your answers will give you only limited insight about your performance—whether you were right or wrong on that particular test.

Checking your answers alone will not give you the kind of insight you need to improve in the future. To improve each time you practice the MPT or MEE, you must figure out recurring mistakes and bad habits—and then fix them. The point sheets and sample answers can't tell you about your own bad habits. Only you can figure those out.

Create a Checklist of Recurring Mistakes

As you take multiple practice exams and evaluate them, you will begin to notice mistakes that you make over and over again. These are your weak points, and you need to turn them into strengths before you take the bar exam.

After you take your first practice MPT or MEE and evaluate it, make a list of everything (everything!) that went wrong. It might feel like a long list. Don't worry about that. Your list should include any mistakes that you noticed while reverse outlining your exam. (Create separate lists for the MPT and the MEE.)

After your second practice MPT or MEE, add to your list of things that went wrong. If something you wrote down after the first practice exam went wrong again, mark it, with a hash mark or other notation. If a problem recurred, you need to know that. Recurring problems are ones that need addressing the most.

Take a third exam. Add to your list of things that went wrong. Now you should be able to spot patterns. Some problems happened only once. Either you were able to fix them right away and they're not problems anymore, or they were one-off goofs that won't happen again. Other problems, though, will have recurred.

For example, on the MPT, you might continuously forget to put in the procedural rule. Or you might forget to include the facts in your point headings. You might forget transition words between rule and application. Whatever your recurring problems are, the most important thing is to discover them— that way, you can fix them. The only way to discover them is to take practice tests and evaluate them.

Reflect on Your Writing Process

We find it immensely helpful to write (short!) reflections on difficult writing tasks. We realize that we are asking you to do more writing after you just did a whole lot of writing. But reflecting (in writing) on a practice test, especially right after you complete the test, is an incredible way to figure out how to improve your test taking skills.

As soon as you finish a practice test, answer these five reflection questions:

1. What was most **difficult** for me about this test and why?
2. How well did I use my **time** and why?
3. What test-taking **strategies** worked best and why?
4. If there were things about this test experience I could instantly **change**, what would they be?
5. What did I do **well** on this test and why?

Type short answers to each of these questions as soon as you finish every practice test, MPT or MEE. The bottom of your document is a fine place for them. Use your answers to help you study for your next practice test. Was time pressure an issue? Figure out what you can do to use your time more wisely. (Review the strategies in Chapter 9, Test-Taking Strategies, and Chapter 10, What If Things Go Wrong?) Did certain strategies work better than others? Pick the ones that worked best and focus on them on your next test.

Notice how your answers change over time as you grow more comfortable taking the MPT and MEE.

C. Give and Receive Peer Feedback

With your writing partner or in your writing group, you should give and receive peer feedback on your practice exams. Giving feedback to another writer not only benefits the person you are giving feedback to, it also benefits you, the person giving the feedback. Noticing errors in another person's writing helps you learn to notice—and avoid—errors in your own writing. Noticing what other writers do well helps you build stronger writing habits.

As a group (or a pair), take the same MPT or MEE. Taking the test together, in the same room, under the same time constraints, helps mimic the environment of the bar exam. You will likely be taking the bar exam with other examinees, so practicing with other test takers—an added distraction—is good practice. If you cannot take the test together in the same room, try to take the test together using online meeting software or a conference call.

Once you are finished, trade your answers, either printed out or digitally. Follow these steps:

(1) **Initial read-through**. Don't read deeply into sentence structure or punctuation. Focus on your response as a reader. What parts are easy to read? What parts aren't? What parts did you have to read multiple times to understand? Do you think the analysis is correct?

(2) **Reverse outline**. Write a reverse outline of your peer's document. Use the annotations in Figure 8.1 in this chapter.

(3) **The weak and the strong**. At the end of your peer's document, write two things that the document needs to improve on and two things that the document does well.

(4) **Discuss**. Give and receive feedback. And as you receive feedback, listen. Don't interrupt. Remember that the feedback isn't personal. As you deliver feedback, remember that there's a person listening to your words, so be gentle with your delivery.

(5) **Use the point sheet or sample answer**. After you have completed your initial peer feedback, review the MPT point sheet or the MEE sample answer. As a team, review how well your answers compare. Help each other interpret the point sheet or sample answer. It's a lot easier if you work together.

(6) **Use your checklists**. Finally, work together to add items to your checklists of recurring mistakes and brainstorm ways to prevent those mistakes in the future.

D. Use MPT Point Sheets

MPT graders use a grading tool called a "point sheet." A point sheet is a narrative description of how the NCBE expects the document to look (the parts of the document that should be included) and the legal points that the document should make. These legal points include rules, application of law to specific facts, conclusions, argument headings, contract clauses, and so on. Point sheets are available at the end of every sample MPT you download from the NCBE website.

Point sheets are only somewhat helpful for assessing your MPT answer. Because a point sheet is narrative in form, rather than, say, a rubric with points assigned to specific content, it is hard to match up what you wrote to what is in the point sheet. The point sheets also don't indicate how much each thing you wrote will be valued. Nevertheless, point sheets are what the NCBE provides as "answer keys" to its MPTs, so let's make the most of them.

Go ahead and download a point sheet now. It will be easier to understand what you are about to read here if you have seen one.

Structure of a Point Sheet

Each point sheet begins with an introduction that describes the task and gives an overview of the legal issues of that MPT. It also tells the grader what was included in the file and library. Finally, the introduction concludes with guidance like this: "The following discussion covers all the points that the drafters of the item intended to raise in the problem."

Next are more overviews. Typically, point sheets include an overview of the task's format (e.g., the parts the task should have and how they should look), an overview of the facts of the file, and/or an overview of the law. This is information that the grader is supposed to use to grade your test.

Point sheets do not have consistent structure, and their parts are often labeled poorly, which makes them difficult to use in your test preparation.

However, **all point sheets contain two things that you should find**: instructions to the grader about what examinees should or should not do, and legal points that the examinee should make when writing their task. Sometimes those points appear in the form of a sample answer. Sometimes they appear as a narrative description. Sometimes they appear as bullets. They can even appear as all three in the same point sheet. Furthermore, instructions for graders are interspersed throughout.

We realize that this description of the point sheet might have filled you with despair. You might be wondering why you should bother writing an organized, coherent, complete MPT answer if it will be judged against a point sheet that we have described as nonsense. If you are feeling this way, your feelings are reasonable. We have had these feelings, too. Here's some solace: MPT graders are real people who take their grading responsibilities seriously, and they will be able to tell if your MPT answer is organized, coherent, and complete, even if the point sheets they receive are not.

Here's some more solace: the next part of this chapter describes how to make the best of this difficult document when evaluating your practice MPTs.

Using a Point Sheet

First, you need to read the point sheet all the way through. Because of the unfortunate organization of point sheets, you can't count on the headings to tell you where valuable information can be found. As you read, use different colored highlighters to highlight these two items:

- Information about how the task should be structured or formatted.
- Instructions to graders about what examinees should do or not do.

What remains unhighlighted should be information about the content of an effective answer or background information for the grader. Usually the background information is concentrated at the beginning of the point sheet. Now you can use the point sheet to evaluate your practice MPT.

Put your annotated task documents next to the first page of the point sheet (either printed out or side-by-side on a computer screen). Compare the point sheet's overview with the annotations you made on your task document. Look at (1) the task name, (2) the task's purpose and audience, and (3) the document's features. What you are doing is seeing how well your genre discovery process aligns with what graders are told that examinees should notice.

Did you notice the right things? If not, make a note in your checklist of recurring mistakes of what went wrong. Did you notice more things than are written in the point sheet? Great, don't worry about that.

Finally, put your completed task next to the point sheet. Skim the parts of the point sheet that you left unhighlighted—the parts that describe the content of an effective answer. Compare this information with your own completed task and evaluate your performance. List any mistakes on your checklist.

E. Use the MEE Sample Answers

The MEE graders use a document called an "Analysis," which is essentially a sample answer. The MEE sample answer is much more straightforward than the MPT point sheet, but it still has its flaws.

One flaw is that the sample answers tend to be far longer than what an ordinary examinee can produce in 30 minutes: it includes multiple single-spaced pages of typed material. You will likely only be able to produce one or two pages. Another flaw is that the sample answers contain an immense amount of law that is densely written, along with legal authorities that are extensively quoted and cited. You may see block quotations that are fifteen lines long, string citations, references to secondary sources, and more. These sorts of rule passages are nothing you could ever produce on the MEE because you do not have a legal research platform inside your brain.

Thus, you need to be savvy when you use the MEE sample answers to evaluate your performance.

Annotate

First, use your case-reading skills from law school to annotate the sample answers by making a reverse outline. The reverse outline of the sample answer will look a lot like a book brief. First, find the blackletter rules contained within the sprawling rule passages. Underline them if you can, or jot down a plain-language version in the margins. Next, find the application passages and label them as such.

Evaluate Rules

Now you can evaluate your own MEE rule passages. Compare the black letter rules you found in the sample answer with the rules in your own answer. The wording need not be the same, but the substance should be. If you missed any parts of the rule, note them in the margins of your answer. You'll refer back to them when you evaluate your application passages.

Evaluate Application

Next, evaluate your application passages. You can spot the application passages in the sample answers because they are (hopefully) set off with transition words like "Here" and do not include legal citations. Each application paragraph probably will not begin with a helpful topic sentence summarizing the point of the paragraph, but you should be able to figure out the point that the paragraph is making. Compare the point of each application paragraph in the sample answer with the point of each of your application paragraphs, which ideally will begin with a helpful topic sentence. (See Appendix 1, Legal Writing under Pressure, for more on paragraphs and topic sentences.) Did you make all of the same points? If not, note the ones you missed or wrote incorrectly. If so, give yourself a high five and start comparing individual facts.

After determining whether the application passages in your answer and the sample answer make the same key points, compare the individual facts that each passage uses. Does your answer rely on the same facts? Does the sample answer include facts that you didn't address? Does each sentence in your answer include a fact you can point to in the fact pattern and a phrase from a rule? Do you write a separate conclusion paragraph that begins, "In conclusion"?

Evaluate Headings

Finally, look at your conclusion headings. Do they state the conclusion proved by the paragraphs that follow? To refresh your memory on how to write strong conclusion headings, see Appendix 1, Legal Writing under Pressure. The conclusion heading is the first thing that the grader will read, so make it easy to understand—make it easy for the grader to give you points.

As you evaluate your MEEs, note any recurring errors on your checklist.

F. Use Bar Prep Company Materials

If you are studying with a bar prep company (e.g., BARBRI or Themis), then you likely received MPT and MEE study materials from them. Great! You would have received materials such as sample tests, sample answers, sample point sheets and answer sheets, and some advice about how to take the tests.

Sometimes these companies will also grade the tests for you and give you feedback. You should definitely make use of this service. One caveat: Don't let their feedback on your exams replace your own judgment of your performance. For each exam you submit to a bar prep company for feedback, you should also do the self-evaluation process described in this chapter.

You should make use of the sample MPTs and MEEs that they give you for practice. Sometimes, the sample tests they give you are not ones that you can easily get elsewhere.

Beware of the bar prep companies' sample answers: Although the sample answers are often complete, they are also often longer than what an ordinary examinee can create in the time allotted for the test. Also, they are not written to be exemplars—that is, they are not perfect. They are a learning tool, but only that. The methods we described for using MPT point sheets and MEE sample answers will work for bar prep company sample answers as well.

Chapter 9

Test-Taking Strategies

The purpose of this chapter is to prepare you for test day by teaching you test-taking strategies. In this chapter, we address potential test surprises so that during the bar exam, you won't be rattled by those surprises.

A. Be Prepared for the Packet

The MPT and MEE are presented to you in test packets. Don't be surprised by the packets you receive on test day.

The MPT Packet

In Chapter 3, What You Need to Know About the MPT, you learned about the MPT test packet. Remember that the test packet comes in one large booklet with both MPTs (MPT-1 and MPT-2) altogether. You will have a three-hour time period to complete both exams. Each exam is designed to take 90 minutes to complete.

You can't separate pages, which means you can't look at the facts alongside the law, or your task documents alongside the rest of the materials. Creating a schematic—essentially a high-concept to-do list of your task—allows you to put information from the task documents into your test software so that you don't have to keep flipping back to your task documents while reading your facts and legal authorities.

Depending on your jurisdiction, you also might not be able to bring flags or other types of bookmarks into the bar exam. For example, as of this writing, the North Carolina bar examiners do not permit examinees to even bring their own pens or pencils; each examinee receives a plastic bag with state-provided writing utensils and earplugs. Moreover, although the MPT instructions say that you will have scratch paper, that scratch paper is stapled into your MPT packet, meaning that you can't rip it into useful bookmarks or use it alongside your test materials.

Thus, at this point in your preparation, you need to research what your jurisdiction allows you to bring into the exam room. If the answer is "nothing" or "not much," then you should plan for that. If, like North Carolina examinees, you have a handful of writing utensils, then you can use them to mark important pages in your packet. Or you can fold the corners of important pages—perhaps the top corners for law and the bottom corners for facts.

The packet also includes the instructions for the MPT, on the outside back cover. You should read these instructions as soon as you receive your packet because, in most cases, you are allowed to read these before the timing starts.

The MEE Packet

The MEE packet is simpler than the MPT packet. (Thank goodness!) If you are in a UBE jurisdiction, you will write six MEE essays in three hours, meaning each essay should take 30 minutes to write.

Each MEE question is one page, single-spaced. (Some run over onto two pages, but only a little, and that is uncommon.) The point is, the questions are short compared to the MPT.

At the top of the question is a fact pattern, and at the bottom are the prompts you must answer in your essay. Most of the prompts are fairly specific—"Were the caller's statements to the 911 dispatcher inadmissible hearsay? Explain." Sometimes the prompts are more vague, like your exams in law school—"Were any crimes committed? Explain."

B. Handling the Time Crunch

One of the most stressful aspects of the bar exam is the time crunch that you will be under when you take the test.

For the MPT, you will receive a packet with two MPTs. Each MPT is designed to take 90 minutes to complete. You will have 180 minutes (three hours) to complete both tests, and you will be responsible for managing your time.

For the MEE, you will receive a packet with six MEEs. Each MEE is designed to take 30 minutes to complete. You will have three hours to complete all six essays, and you will be responsible for managing your time.

For some of you, even thinking about these testing scenarios is stressful. Here are some strategies you can put in place now to relieve the stress of the time crunch.

Use Genre Discovery for the MPT

The default advice for taking the MPT, or even for doing practical legal writing, is to read all the materials (facts and law) first, draft an outline, and then draft your document. *You do not have time to do your MPT in this fashion.* Instead, you should take notes and draft your task while you are reading your MPT materials. Your schematic makes it possible for you to do so.

Everything you learned earlier in this book is designed to help you deal with the time crunch, including genre discovery. By using the task documents to create a schematic, you make it easier to write your task as you read your file and library. Writing-as-you-read is far more efficient than reading everything in your packet and then starting to write afterward.

Your genre discovery schematic outlines the entire document first so that you can write your answer *while you read* the facts and law. You will likely have to review the material some as you finish writing your answer, but you will not have to read the packet over and over. The schematic tells you what you are looking for as you read *before* you start reading.

Note: The first time you took a practice MPT, you may have read the packet all the way through before you started typing. The first time the authors of this book took practice MPTs, we did the same thing. This is a sensible way to familiarize yourself with a new kind of test. From now on, take your practice MPTs using a schematic and the other strategies you learned in this book.

Make Decisions Ahead of Time

The more test-day decisions you can make ahead of time—before you walk into the building to take the test—the faster you will be able to take the test. Making decisions ahead of time can also reduce stress on test day.

Some decisions we have already encouraged you to make include these:

(1) To use a pen or pencil, not a highlighter, to annotate your tests.
(2) To write a schematic for both the MPT and the MEE.
(3) To type important facts and law into your schematic as you read the MPT file and library or the MEE fact pattern.
(4) To write informal MPT citations, if you need them, and no MEE citations.

(5) To use default transition words or phrases that you have memorized in advance.

For the MPT specifically, we have encouraged you to make these decisions:

(1) To complete MPT-1 before MPT-2.
(2) To mark important pages in your MPT test packet by folding corners.
(3) To choose whether to read the law library first, or the facts first, or to have a strategy for choosing which to read first.

For the MEE specifically, we have encouraged you to make this decision:

(1) To read the MEE questions before reading the MEE fact pattern.

Here are some other decisions you can make ahead of time. You should make these decisions when you practice taking exams.

How you plan to divide your time. After you have practiced the MPT and the MEE multiple times, you should have a sense for how long it takes you to do the different test-taking steps. As you take practice MPTs, pay attention to how long it takes you to read the task documents, create your schematic, and so on. Once you have good data, you should map out a plan and practice that plan for how you will use your time on test day.

For the MEE, you only have 30 minutes to write you answer, so be sure you have a plan for how to apportion your time. We suggest considering your time in five-minute chunks. If you can, set aside a few minutes at the end to write strong conclusions and check for any gaps in your rules or analysis.

How you will annotate your test documents. For example, you might use "Example" to indicate an example from a case (also called a rule illustration or case illustration) and "A" for application. (See Chapter 8, Evaluate Your Practice Tests, for a list of margin annotations.)

Learn to Type Faster

Quite simply, the faster that you can type, the faster you can complete your exams. If you are a slow typist, you need to increase your typing speed. Ideally, your typing would be able to keep pace with your thinking.[1] Furthermore, hav-

---

1. "[T]he average [is] 30–40 word-per-minute (WPM)" as opposed to "60–80 WPM," which is perhaps about the speed necessary to keep up with your thoughts." Jessica Brown, "One Skill to Make You Type a Lot Faster," Apr. 23, 2018, BBC.com, https://www.bbc.com/worklife/article/20180423-one-skill-to-make-you-type-a-lot-faster.

ing confidence in your typing speed will help you feel relaxed about the time you spend planning your test answers.

To increase your typing speed, you first need to figure out how fast you type. Go take an online typing test. As of this printing, the website Typing.com provided a good test, free of charge. If you are typing 40 words per minute or slower, see if you can improve your typing speed by 10 to 20 words per minute before you take the bar exam.

There are many online games or downloadable apps that will teach you how to type. Many of these are free. As of this printing, Typing.com provided free student accounts with lessons and games to improve typing speed.

Improving your typing speed is a reasonable task to accomplish in a matter of weeks. But it is not something you can do if the bar exam is next week. Start improving your typing speed as soon as you can.

◊ Hot Tip

The bar exam is not the only reason you should increase your typing speed. The average person types 30–40 words per minute, while professional typists type much faster. But what is a "professional typist" in the legal profession? If you are just starting out as a lawyer, and you are the most junior attorney in your firm, you will be expected to do your own typing—and possibly the typing for your supervisor. It is rare for a junior attorney to have the support of a paralegal or legal secretary. And if you are in a small or solo firm, you might not have the support of a legal secretary, ever. The "professional typist" in the legal profession, therefore, will be *you*. Typing fast is thus not only a **test-taking skill**, but also a **lawyering skill**. Long after you take the bar exam, you will need to be a strong typist. Gain the skill now and thank yourself later.

C. Learn Your Core Genres

When you walk into the testing room to take your exam, you must have expertise in the three core genres: office memo, brief, and letter. If you can't write the three core genres with confidence, you need to review Chapters 4, 5, and 6 (which address the office memo, brief, and letter). If you have a study group, you can practice together.

As you learned in Chapter 7, when you write your MEE, you are writing a similar genre to your law school essays, a genre that is familiar to you already: legal analysis essays that use C-RAC structure.

D. Practice Your Exams

The more practice tests you can take ahead of time, the better. As you practice the MPT and the MEE, you will become better at performing the strategies you need to do well. With practice, on the MEE, you will be able to identify pertinent facts more quickly and write rule paragraphs with greater confidence. As you practice the MPT, creating schematics and using them to write documents will become second nature—and that will make you a better legal writer forever, not just on the MPT.

Here are some strategies that will help you effectively practice taking the MPT and MEE.

Software: Practice using focus mode in Microsoft Word, full-screen mode in Apple Pages (with the inspector window turned off), or full-screen mode in Google Docs. These modes will better simulate the stripped-down writing situation you will use in your exam software.

Writing Tools: All jurisdictions limit what you can bring into the test room with you, but some jurisdictions are extremely restrictive. Learn ahead of time what writing implements you can use on test day, and practice with them.

Time Constraints: When you practice the MPT or MEE, use a timing device, and be strict about time. Time pressure is a major factor on the bar exam, and you should mimic it when you practice. Sometimes, you should practice under a time constraint that is shorter than you will have on bar exam day: take the MPT in 75 minutes, for example. Take an MEE in 20 minutes. This added time pressure will make the full time duration seem much easier.

Self-Evaluation: We dedicated Chapter 8, Evaluate Your Practice Tests, to teaching you how to evaluate your own practice tests and improve your performance. It's not enough just to take practice tests. You need to evaluate your work and transfer what you learned to future tests so that you can improve. We also encourage you to form a study group and to review each other's practice exams. It's often easier to evaluate someone else's work than your own. Plus, seeing how other people wrote the same exam can expand your own writing repertoire.

E. Disability Accommodations

Although the NCBE creates the test components for the Uniform Bar Exam, it does not determine disability accommodations. Instead, your individual jurisdiction determines them. One thing is certain: If you have disability accommodations in law school, you can't count on those same accommodations being available to you when you take the bar exam.

If you need testing accommodations on the bar exam, you should apply for them as early as you can in your 3L year. The website for your jurisdiction will have information about how to apply for those accommodations. The earlier you start, the more time you will have to submit more information if the bar examiners request it. You will also have time to make mistakes in your application (which are okay to make) and to fix them.

If you need help with your application for accommodations, talk to your law school's dean of students. If you need additional help, the dean of students office can help you find a disability attorney to assist you.

Note: The American Bar Association Commission on Disability Rights has created a resource titled "Bar Information for Applicants with Disabilities" (BIAD), located on the ABA website.[2]

---

2. The American Bar Association Commission on Disability Rights, "Bar Information for Applicants with Disabilities," https://www.americanbar.org/groups/diversity/disability rights/resources/biad/.

Chapter 10

What If Things Go Wrong?

The purpose of this chapter is to help you problem-solve, in advance, the possible challenges that might arise when you write for the bar. This chapter is set up like a frequently asked questions (FAQ) page on a website.

When you are done reading this chapter, you will likely think of even more questions. Good! Make a list of any other questions that you have about test day that we haven't answered, and then find answers for them, too, before the test.

Remember: the more problems you can solve before test day, the easier it will be to write strong MPT and MEE answers.

A. What if I don't understand the MPT task?

Before you take the MPT, you will not know what tasks you will be assigned. The purpose of this book is to teach you how to approach any possible MPT task, no matter what the genre is. However, as we've discussed throughout this book, there are two things you must do in advance to ensure that you understand your assigned task: you must be confident writing the MPT core genres, and you must be able to use genre discovery to write an MPT task.

Recall that the three core genres are the office memo, the brief, and the letter. (See Chapters 4, 5, and 6.) You must be confident writing these three genres before test day. When you are assigned these genres on the MPT, you will likely receive little instruction for how to write them in the task documents.

The task documents may not even call them by familiar names. Therefore, you need to be so familiar with these genres that you can pick up on their characteristics by the gestures the task memo makes in their general direction. For example, you need to know that "write me a brief for the judge to support our motion" refers to a trial brief, even though the task document never used the words "trial brief."

For rarer tasks, ones that you likely aren't confident writing, the MPT provides more guidance in how to write your task. For these tasks, you need to be able to use genre discovery to analyze your task documents and write your schematic. Together, genre discovery and your schematic will coach you through your task for your unfamiliar genre.

In short, if you prepare the way we've described in this book—using genre discovery on your task documents—you *will* understand the task.

B. What if I don't understand the law on my MPT?

At this point in your bar preparation, you have taken multiple practice MPTs. You have encountered the case law, statutory law, and other kinds of legal authorities that the MPT uses to test your practical legal writing skills. If, by chance, you haven't taken multiple practice MPTs under time pressure, you need to go do so. You need to understand how the legal authorities are presented on the MPT. That is, they are edited down to just the parts that you need. Every authority serves a purpose, and there are few, if any, red herrings. Your job is to figure out which parts go where.

If you don't understand a judicial opinion, don't panic. You've been reading confusing judicial opinions for three years now during law school. Remind yourself that you know what you're doing. The problem is likely *not* that the opinion is confusing. The problem is likely that you are nervous because it is test day. So, if you are reading and the words are confusing, skim ahead until you reach a part of the opinion that is easy to understand. Read that part first and get comfortable with the opinion. Then go back to the beginning and read it again.

If there are particular words in the law that you don't understand, first look for context clues that help you understand their meaning. But also look in other authorities and see if the words are defined elsewhere in the law library. If a word is important to the task, then other authorities will use it, too. If it isn't, they won't, and you can forget about it.

If a statute is confusing, once again, don't panic. The first thing you need to do is read the entire statute. Don't stop reading until you reach the end. Then, go back to the beginning and use your pen or pencil and divide the statute into chunks of information. Annotate it in the margins, noting general rules, exceptions, definitions, and other important sections. Circle verbs, conjunctions, and limiters (e.g., only, unless, not, never). After you have annotated your statute, it will be less overwhelming. (For more help on understanding law, see Appendix 2, Legal Reading under Pressure.)

C. What if I can't figure out a structure to use?

For the MPT, the structure that you use to write your task is tied to the schematic that you create, which is tied to the genre of your task. If you aren't sure what structure to use on the MPT, stop and take a deep breath. You know the process of figuring out how to structure your MPT task. Genre discovery gives you a methodical approach to do so. Go back to your task documents and figure out your task's name, audience, and purpose. Then, use genre discovery to create your schematic. (To review genre discovery, see Chapter 3, How to Take the MPT).

For MEE essays, you are writing legal analysis essays that use C-RAC structure (similar to your law school exam essays). You will also use conclusion headings to separate each section of your analysis. Fortunately, you are already familiar with this legal analysis structure because you learned it in your 1L legal writing course, and you've been using it on your practice tests.

If you are *not* familiar with C-RAC structure, organization of legal analysis, conclusion headings, or other legal writing techniques you need for bar writing, review Appendix 1, Legal Writing under Pressure.

D. What if I get stuck?

You may get stuck while you are writing an MPT task or an MEE essay. The best way to prevent this from happening is to practice taking these exams. The more you practice, the more you will encounter test pressure and the situations that cause you to get stuck: you forget the law, you don't understand the task, etc. These problems happen, and you want to encounter them for the first time in practice, not on exam day.

Here are some tips for how to help you keep your fingers typing on exam day (or under any time-crunch writing situation in law school or law practice).

Don't Stop Writing

"Don't stop writing" might seem like obvious advice, but it is harder than it sounds. As you take your practice tests, notice every time your fingers freeze on the keyboard. Every time you stop writing, even for a moment, notice. Try to keep count by drawing a hash mark on a piece of paper. How many times did you pause? How many times did you run out of words?

Of course I'm going to need to stop, you might argue. You'll need to ponder. You'll need to make sure you're saying something that makes sense.

Actually, not really. You don't need to ponder—because you planned. On the MPT, you wrote a schematic, and on that schematic, you wrote down all of your pondering. If you aren't typing, then you are reading. If you aren't reading, then you are typing.

On the MEE, if you aren't typing, you are probably racking your brain trying to remember the law. Don't do that. Instead, start typing everything you can think of that has anything to do with the law that applies to your fact pattern. (We describe this process in greater detail in Chapter 7, The MEE Bar Essays.) List everything you can remember about the law. Rather than staring at the question like a terrified rabbit, worrying about what law you don't know, type the law that you do know. Give yourself two minutes. Type a free-association list of legal concepts that might have anything to do with the law of your fact pattern. See what emerges. Something might. Something probably will. If something does, delete what you typed to get you there, and get working.

If nothing emerges, make up some law using your common sense, and keep going. At least you did your best.

While writing your MPT and MEE application passages, you need to keep writing as well. Take every determinative fact and use it in your application. Make sure that for each fact you use, you pair it with law. On the MEE, where you don't have a lot of law to work with, you might feel like you are being repetitive with the law. You probably are! That's fine. Don't worry. Apply that smidgen of law to the facts over and over again until you've used up all of the relevant facts.

The point is, do not stop writing.

But what if your brain is fried? What if what you're writing isn't your best work? We have an answer for that, too.

The Eighty Percent Draft

We'd like to introduce you to the concept of the **80% draft**. The 80% draft is a method that we, as co-authors,[1] use to write documents quickly. The idea of the 80% draft is that the first author of a draft writes the draft as quickly as possible, aiming for 80%: 80% completion, 80% quality, and 80% of any other measure of goodness that you can think of.

This first author lets go of perfectionism, because the goal isn't perfection, it is only 80%. The author leaves the final 20% in the hands of her co-author. Letting go of that final 20% is incredibly freeing. It allows you to write very quickly because your sentences do not have to be perfect. Your ideas come more quickly because you do not judge how you write them down. Your only goal is to get your ideas down, period. You trust that someone else will come along after you to make your ideas beautiful.

If you are co-authoring a book or a brief or any other document in the future, we highly recommend using the 80% draft method.

On the bar exam, you do not have a co-author who will come behind you to beautify your work. But your goal should be an 80% draft. If you let go of that final 20%—the perfect word, the elegant sentence, the exact statement of the rule—then you will get much more writing done. Best of all, you will be far less likely to encounter writer's block, which is caused by perfectionism and fear.

Write an 80% draft, a good-enough draft. That's all you need.

E. What if I'm running out of time?

The MPT and MEE evaluate your ability to work under pressure and in a time crunch. Time is one of the constraints. In other words, you should expect to run out of time going in to both the MPT and the MEE. Given that you are likely going to run out of time, you need to plan for it.

For the MPT, you need to be sure that you set aside time for both of your MPTs. You need to be sure that you start writing your schematic as soon as you open your packet, instead of reading all the way through your packet and forgetting to start typing. You need to take a lot of practice MPTs so that you

---

1. Author Katie Rose Guest Pryal first used the 80% draft method with her co-author Jordynn Jack, Ph.D., when writing *How Writing Works: A Guide to Composing Genres* (Oxford University Press, 2015).

develop good MPT habits (habits that will, after the MPT, serve you well in law practice).

For the MEE, you only have 30 minutes to write each of your answers, so be sure you have a plan for how to apportion your time. If you can, set aside a few minutes at the end to write strong conclusions and check for any gaps in your rules or analysis.

On test day, as time starts to run down on your exam answers, don't worry. And whatever you do, do *not* stop typing. Don't try to find the perfect word or sentence. Type words that make sense even if they are sentences you would never turn in to a boss or judge. It's better to have an answer to a legal question than no answer at all. We give you permission to write some truly terrible sentences under the time pressure of the bar exam.

One of the legal writing skills that you will learn as you train for and take the bar exam is the ability to write a fast first draft. Ideally, in practice, you will have time to revise that first draft. But training for the bar exam will ease you out of any writer's block you may have developed in your working life. Defeating writer's block is a major professional accomplishment!

So, as time runs down on the bar exam, you will write words, sometimes crappy words, that complete your writing task. And you will not stop typing those words until time is called. And you won't be surprised by the time crunch because you will have prepared for it.

F. What if I freak out on test day?

If you walk into the exam room and freak out, which is a possibility, you will use the strategies that you have practiced in advance of the exam to calm yourself.

What strategies? If you don't have them, then you need them. Even the most experienced competitor, or performer, or test taker can freeze under pressure. There is always a chance, even if you practice a lot. So prepare for freezing (or freaking out, or choking).

First, you need to be able to notice that you are freaking out. Second, you need to have a plan *before* test day in case you do. Try these strategies:

Deep breathing. Take five deep breaths. Count to three (in your head) as you breathe in, and count to four (in your head) as you breathe out. It's possible that you will be breathing fast when you start deep breathing, and that's okay. Keep repeating until you have control over your breathing. That's the point.

Create a slogan or good-luck drawing. Before test day, create a kind phrase, something encouraging that you can say to yourself whenever you are struggling. Or, draw a cute or funny picture for yourself, something simple, but that triggers happiness. You need to create these in advance of test day. On test day, draw or write these happiness triggers on your test booklet to lift you up.

5-4-3-2-1. This exercise makes you use all five of your senses to help you calm down. Use each of your five senses to spot five things. You **see** five things and name them (in your head). You **touch** four things (your pencil, the back of your hand, your desk, your laptop). You **hear** three things. You **smell** two things. And you **taste** one thing (like the roof of your mouth). This exercise works because you can't do it and also be stuck in your panicky head.[2]

Try these strategies out and see if one works for you. If it does, practice it under pressure when you are taking a practice exam. If none of them work for you, find one that does.

G. What if I fail the bar exam?

Some people fail the bar. If you look at bar passage rates, you could say that a *lot* of people fail the bar. In fact, Katie Pryal, one of the authors of this book, failed the bar—it's one of the reasons that she wanted to write this book. She failed the bar, clerked for a federal judge, passed the bar, and then became a law professor. So the short answer is, if you fail the bar, you'll take it again and pass, and then you'll tell people that you failed the bar so that they won't worry as much about taking the bar—or feel so badly if they fail it, too.

In more practical terms, if you fail the bar, you will make a plan for how to pass it. You will reach out to a mentor at your law school, perhaps your legal writing professor (that's what Professor Pryal did), and ask that person to help you. You will find out whether the board of law examiners in your state allows examinees who fail the bar to look at their exams (some do). You and your mentor will go and look at your exam to see where things went awry. Then, you will take that information and figure out how to study better for the next bar exam. Your mentor will help you find better resources, even if that means referring you to someone who can better help you.

You will not feel ashamed. You will not think you are stupid or unworthy of being a lawyer. You will not give up.

---

2. We owe this exercise to Ellen Hendriksen and her book *How to Be Yourself: Quiet Your Inner Critic and Rise Above Social Anxiety* (2018).

H. What if I can't stop worrying?

Too much worrying is not good for you. You need to study for the bar exam, yes, but you also need to take care of yourself. You need to eat, sleep, and have fun—and study for the bar.

If you find that you are worrying so much that the worry interferes with eating, sleeping, or having fun, then you are worrying an unhealthy amount, and you need help. You need to get help immediately, or you will hurt your chances of passing the bar.

If you feel so depressed or worried that you might hurt yourself, put down this book and call 911 immediately.

If your law school has a bar prep or academic support program (ASP) to support you while you study for the bar, start by reaching out to them—or another professor at your law school whom you trust. **Tell them, honestly, that your worry over the bar is interfering with your health.** Don't lie or try to play it down. Your law school's ASP team will know how to help you, but only if you're honest with them. They want you to succeed. Let them help you.

I. What if I have more questions?

You *will* need more advice! That's why you have a group of friends, teachers, and supporters around you to help. We've encouraged you to form a writing group (even if you only have one other person in your group), and that person is someone you can turn to for advice and ideas. Reach out to your academic support program (ASP) at your law school for mentorship and guidance. If you're still close with other mentors from law school, turn to them for advice if you need it. Build yourself a support system and use it.

Appendix 1

Legal Writing under Pressure

The purpose of this appendix is to teach you how to write legal analysis in high-pressure situations such as the bar exam. Here, we will present best practices for writing legal analysis in *all* situations, and we will also flag tips for how to maximize your writing speed under pressure.

Legal analysis is the process of applying law to facts to draw a legal conclusion. The most important tool you need to write legal analysis is C-RAC, the method of legal reasoning and communicating legal analysis that lawyers use.

C-RAC is an acronym that stands for conclusion, rules, application, and conclusion. The Golden Rule of legal logic — explain the law before you apply the law — helps you understand C-RAC structure. You already learned C-RAC in law school (although you might have called it something different, such as CREAC or IRAC), and this chapter will help you remember how to use it.

Being able to quickly use C-RAC is an important **legal writing skill** for law school and law practice. It is also an important **test-taking skill** for the bar exam. On the MPT, you will use C-RAC whether you are assigned a memo, brief, or letter (the core MPT genres), or a bench memo, judicial opinion, trial court order, or complaint (some of the rare MPT genres from past bar exams). In our research of past MPTs, there has never been an MPT assigned where examinees did not need to use C-RAC. On the MEE, you will use C-RAC to write each of your essays.

In addition to C-RAC, this appendix reviews other core legal writing topics, such as large-scale organization, headings, paragraphs, topic sentences, transitions, and citations.

A. C-RAC: The Basic Structure of Legal Analysis

To present legal analysis to readers, lawyers use C-RAC. C-RAC is the conventional structure of legal analysis that legal readers—including your bar exam graders—expect to see. C-RAC is an acronym for the basic parts of legal analysis: conclusion, rules, application, and conclusion. You use one C-RAC to analyze one legal issue. An **issue** is a point in dispute that needs to be resolved by legal analysis.

C-RAC is the basic building block of legal analysis. In fact, no matter how long and winding your legal analysis gets, C-RAC is your *only* building block. A legal analysis can be as short as one sentence if the law applies directly to the facts. Or, a legal analysis can be tens of pages long when the law doesn't apply directly to the facts, and the writer must use a lot of words to make the law do so.

For the purposes of C-RAC, **rule** means the law you use in your analysis. **Application** is the part of legal analysis in which you match law to your facts to draw a legal conclusion. And a **conclusion** succinctly states what happens when you apply the law to your facts.

"Conclusion" appears twice in C-RAC—at the end and at the beginning. Legal readers expect to see the conclusion of an analysis *before* they begin reading so that they can assess whether the analysis supports a conclusion while they read. In many legal genres, that initial conclusion appears in a **conclusion heading** (also called a point heading or an argument heading). Later in this chapter, you will learn how to write conclusion headings. Conclusion headings are important for both the MPT and the MEE.

B. Large-Scale Organization (Sections and Subsections)

Sometimes, when you write legal analysis, you only need to write one C-RAC. This happens when there is only one legal issue that you need to resolve. Alas, such simple legal analysis is rare. It is certainly rare on the MPT. This section discusses two different types of complex organization schemes that you might need to use in your legal writing (in practice and on the bar exam).

Branching Analysis: Elements and Factors

Sometimes you have to write an analysis of a legal issue that is made up of multiple sub-issues. For example, if the law of your MPT provides an elements test or a factor test, you might need separate C-RACs for each element or factor. **A legal issue made up of sub-issues is best analyzed by breaking your analysis into sub-analyses with separate C-RACs.** If your legal analysis had sub-analyses, you will use subsections to divide your analysis.

🔥 *Hot Tip*

Figuring out how to break a legal analysis into sub-analyses is an important **legal writing skill**. On the MPT and MEE, it is also an important **test-taking skill**. On the bar exam, you will sometimes be given the structure of your analysis: Your quirky MPT boss might tell you to analyze three specific sub-issues, or an MEE question might contain two specific prompts. But even if the exam does not tell you specifically which issues to analyze, you likely still will need subsections in your analysis. If the MPT task memo or MEE prompts don't tell you, how do you figure out how to organize your subsections?

On the MPT, you look to the law in the library. The cases or statutes will have "elements," "factors," "prongs," or "steps." Use these rule parts to organize the subsections of your analysis. Each rule part receives its own sub-analysis. Sometimes, the rule parts in the law suggest a different organization than the one that your quirky boss assigned. In those situations, **always do what your quirky boss says.**[1]

On the MEE, if the prompts don't provide organization for your analysis, the law or the facts will provide it for you. If the prompt is one large, vague question, do your best to break it into two or three sub-questions that you can analyze separately.

When you need to analyze a legal issue by breaking it into sub-issues, use **branching analysis structure.** A branching analysis is useful when a rule has

---

1. Some MPT point sheets include alternative large-scale organizations that graders should accept as correct. Some don't. The quirky boss's organization is always correct—after all, using it shows that you can follow directions, an important lawyering and test-taking skill. If you can't easily write your answer using your quirky boss's structure, but you can easily write an answer using a branching analysis, do what you need to do to write your document in the time allotted.

multiple parts and two or more of those rule parts require separate legal analyses. In a branching analysis, you break down your analysis of your main legal issue into two or more sub-analyses, each with a separate C-RAC. For example, imagine that your main legal issue is whether a contract was formed between two parties. The parties agree that there was an offer, but they disagree as to whether there was acceptance and consideration. To resolve your main legal issue, you must first resolve the two sub-issues of acceptance and consideration. To write your analysis of the contract dispute, you need to write a branching analysis, with one C-RAC for the acceptance sub-issue and another for the consideration sub-issue. Your legal analysis, as a whole, is of one set of facts and one legal issue, but the sub-issues of acceptance and consideration must be analyzed separately with their own C-RACs.

The two most common types of rules that use branching analysis are elements tests and factor tests. An **elements test** is a rule that contains elements. An **element** is one part of a rule that *must* be proven in order for a claim to succeed. In other words, each element is a requirement. Legal authorities usually explicitly state the elements that make up elements tests. You can spot an elements test when the court uses language of requirement, like "must" or "shall" or "requires."

Unlike elements, factors are not determinative. A **factor** is a fact or condition that may *contribute* to a particular outcome but does not *determine* the outcome. (You can think of a factor as a dimmer, in contrast to an element's on/off switch.) A **factor test** is a rule that contains factors. Factor tests are also sometimes called **balancing tests**, **weighing tests**, and **totality-of-the-circumstances tests**. Regardless, when legal writers apply factor tests, they don't have to prove all of the factors. Instead, they analyze the merits of different factors and then, *considering the factors together*, they draw conclusions. Verbs like "consider" or "weigh" or "examine" often indicate factor tests.

Noticing that a test is an elements test or factor test will allow you to quickly determine that the most appropriate large-scale organization is a branching analysis. A branching structure works well for issues that have sub-issues. But what's the best way to organize an analysis that has several distinct issues?

Multi-Issue Analysis: Distinct Legal Issues

Sometimes you need to analyze two (or more) distinct legal issues from your case in one document. These issues might rely on unrelated law and even on unrelated facts from your case. Or these issues might rely on similar law and similar facts, but each is a distinct question that must be addressed separately.

In any case, neither issue relies on the other issue for resolution. In fact, the only thing they might have in common is that they arose in the same case.

For example, a court opinion might address an appeal of two issues. One issue on appeal might be an evidentiary error and another might be a sentencing error. These unrelated errors on appeal both need to be analyzed in one document, but each issue must be analyzed separately, with entirely separate C-RACs. They share no rules; the C-RACs do not branch from a common legal test.

In instances such as these, you have a multi-issue analysis, and you should use a **multi-issue analysis structure**. A multi-issue analysis structure is an analysis structure that resolves more than one distinct issue within the same document. You should approach each issue separately, with a separate C-RAC.

When using a multi-issue analysis structure, your large-scale organization will be multiple C-RACs, each with a numbered conclusion heading. The sample office memo in Chapter 4 of this book shows an example of a multi-issue analysis structure.

Regardless of how your analysis is organized, each section or subsection that you write will need its own conclusion heading. Read on for how to write them.

◊ Hot Tip

Sometimes in your legal writing, one (or more) of your separate issues in a multi-issue analysis might need a branching analysis. In fact, it is a common structure of MPT tasks that we studied for there to be two issues for analysis, and for one of those issues to be branching.

C. Conclusion Headings

A conclusion heading is a heading that concisely summarizes a legal analysis's conclusion. Conclusion headings are written and punctuated as sentences.[2] They are sometimes called point headings or argument headings.

Legal readers want to immediately know the conclusion you are drawing in your analysis so that they can evaluate your analysis while they read it.

---

2. For more about conclusion headings, see Alexa Z. Chew and Katie Rose Guest Pryal, *The Complete Legal Writer* 345 (2nd ed. 2020).

Therefore, they want to know the conclusion of your legal analysis at the *beginning* of your analysis. Present this conclusion in a concise heading. Your conclusion heading should state the thing that you are proving by applying the applicable law to the determinative facts.

Here are strategies for writing conclusion headings. You will use similar strategies to write the brief answer for an office memo, or even the first paragraph in a letter.

Basic Structure

A conclusion heading is composed of three things: (1) law, (2) facts, and (3) the legal conclusion you draw when you apply the law to the facts.

Here is a common template for how to craft conclusion headings. Although you can be creative in how you write your headings, when you are under pressure, a template comes in handy:

Under _____ [law], _____ [phrase that states conclusion], when _____ [facts].

Or simply remember this: Under-Does-When.

🔥 Hot Tip

Throughout this appendix you will see "templates" for various legal writing conventions, like conclusion headings, rule examples, and roadmaps. Under pressure, templates are helpful shortcuts to getting the necessary words onto the page in an understandable order. When you have more time to write, you can and should consider your sentences more thoughtfully.

Here's how it works in practice. Say your town has an ordinance that says that apartment landlords cannot ban tenants from keeping certain breeds of dogs; they can ban all dogs or no dogs. Your firm's client was evicted from her apartment after she adopted a "pit-bull-type dog," and her landlord gave the dog as the reason for her eviction in an email. Your boss wants to know whether the landlord's actions likely violated the law.

Based on what we know right now, you can write this conclusion heading in a memo to your boss:

Under the town's ordinance forbidding landlords from banning breeds of dogs, the landlord's actions **do** violate the law, **when** the landlord told the tenant in writing she was evicted because of the breed of her dog.

Let's look at this conclusion heading broken out into a list of its parts:

Law: Under the town's ordinance forbidding landlords from banning breeds of dogs,
Conclusion: the landlord's actions do violate the law,
Facts: when the landlord told the tenant in writing she was evicted because of the breed of her dog.

In this particular conclusion heading, the order of the statements is law-conclusion-fact. (Indeed, that's the order of Under-Does-When.) But you can write your conclusion headings with your statements in any order—so long as you have all three parts.

For example, you can often use the word "because" in place of "when" in a conclusion heading. In fact, you can use "because" a lot in conclusion headings, stringing them together if you need to.

The landlord's actions **do** violate the law **because** the town's ordinance forbids landlords from banning breeds of dogs, and the landlord told the tenant in writing she was evicted **because** of the breed of her dog.

In this manifestation of the conclusion heading, the conclusion comes first, the law second, and the facts last.

On the MPT and MEE, you will need to write conclusion headings that are very easy for your reader to understand, and you will need to write them quickly. Your graders will likely skim your work, and what they will see first, and most, are your conclusion headings. Make sure your headings are excellent. One way to ensure that you are able to write excellent headings is to make sure you know the various parts of headings well. Can you tell what's missing if you see an incomplete heading?

Incomplete Headings

Let's look at the various parts of a conclusion heading more closely and learn how to spot incomplete conclusion headings. Here is another example of an effective conclusion heading:

Summary judgment for Defendant is appropriate because Plaintiffs' nuisance claim is based on the acts of wild animals, which cannot create a nuisance as a matter of law.

Let's break out the three parts of this conclusion heading: the conclusion, the facts, and the law.

> **Conclusion:** Summary judgment for Defendant is appropriate because
> **Facts:** Plaintiffs' nuisance claim is based on the acts of wild animals,
> **Law:** which cannot create a nuisance as a matter of law.

Now, these three parts of a conclusion heading can appear in any order. Recall that in the Under-Does-When template, "Under" refers to the law, so the law comes first. But the law doesn't have to come first for a conclusion heading to be great.

Let's return to our nuisance conclusion heading. It has all three parts: conclusion, facts, and law. Compare it to the one that follows. The following example is incomplete because it omits the facts of the case; although the heading talks about wild animals, those are animals in the abstract, not the ones at issue *in this case*:

> Summary judgment for Defendant is appropriate because wild animals cannot create a nuisance as a matter of law.

And below is a conclusion heading that is incomplete because it omits the applicable law, which is about the relationship between wild animals and the law of nuisance:

> Summary judgment for Defendant is appropriate because Plaintiff's nuisance claim is based on the acts of wild animals.

A complete legal conclusion includes both the facts and the law, so be sure your conclusion headings include both. Note also that you can use this same strategy to write other document parts such as questions presented, brief answers, and appellate brief issue statements.

D. Rule Passages

There are only two kinds of rules. First, there are rules of general applicability. Second, there are rule examples (sometimes called "rule illustrations") that describe the application of a rule in a specific precedent. Here's how you'll use these two kinds of rules in your legal analysis.

Rules of General Applicability

A rule of general applicability is a rule that applies to a variety of factual situations. You can find these rules in cases, statutes, and regulations. Here is an example from the fictional jurisdiction of Rhode Hampshire, cited using MPT citation style:

> Taking a large, valuable livestock animal, whose fiber has significant commercial value, can be a Class H felony. *State v. Bosley* (R.H. Sup. Ct. 2005).

In this example, the rule is a criminal law rule (e.g., "felony"), is taken from case law (e.g., "*State v. Bosley*"), and describes a very particular kind of crime. Even though the description of the crime is detailed, it is still a rule of general applicability—this is not the description of how this rule was applied in a particular case. This is the rule you would use if you encountered a factual situation in which a livestock animal with valuable hair fiber was stolen, an animal such as an alpaca, or a mohair goat, or a vicuña.

To write a paragraph with a rule of general applicability, begin with a straightforward statement of the rule. Sometimes, before the rule, you can write a default phrase that conveys generality, such as "in general." Then, after you state the broadest general rule, state any more rules of general applicability that narrow the scope of the rule, funneling from broadest to narrow. (We talk more about funneling later in this section.)

Here's an example of a rule of general applicability paragraph that uses informal MPT citation style:

> In general, a private nuisance occurs "when one makes an improper use of his own property and in that way injures the land or some incorporeal right of one's neighbor." *Morgan v. High Penn Oil Co.* (N.C. Sup. Ct. 1953). To recover for private nuisance, a plaintiff must prove two elements: (1) the defendant used its own property in such a way as to "unreasonably ... interfere[] with the plaintiff's use and enjoyment of the plaintiff's property" and (2) the defendant's unreasonable invasion or interference caused substantial injury to the plaintiff. *Elliott v. Muehlbach* (N.C. Ct. App. 2005) (citing *Watts v. Pama Mfg. Co.* (N.C. 1962)).

Here is the same example, but written as you might write it on the MEE—without quotations and citations:

> In general, a private nuisance occurs when a person improperly uses her own property in such a way that she injures the land or her neighbor's right to use his land. Private nuisance has two elements: (1) the defendant used her property in a way that unreasonably interfered with a neighboring plaintiff's use and enjoyment of his property and (2) the defendant's unreasonable interference substantially injured the plaintiff.

Both versions of this rule paragraph open with a topic sentence stating the general rule, which is obvious from the default phrase "in general." Both versions of the paragraph then funnel from broad to narrow, ending with the two-element test that the writer will apply in the analysis.

Procedural Rules

A procedural rule or standard is a type of rule of general applicability. Procedural rules are court rules that tell courts how to apply the substantive law to analyze issues—they tell you what to do with your law. In legal practice and on the bar exam, you will likely be asked to answer procedural questions, such as "whether a charge should be dismissed" or "whether summary judgment should be granted." To answer these questions, you will need to know your jurisdiction's rule governing the dismissal of a criminal charge or the granting of summary judgment.

Procedural rules govern trial briefs, appellate briefs, and judicial opinions. The rules originate in the court rules of a jurisdiction and are explained by case law. For example, if you are writing a trial-level document, you will use a trial standard.

◉ Hot Tip

Trial briefs usually ask a judge to make a decision on a matter of procedure—like granting summary judgment or excluding evidence—and thus trial briefs typically include a procedural passage that describes the relevant rules. Knowing about procedural standards is an important **lawyering skill**.

Recognizing procedural standards is also an important **test-taking skill**. If the authorities in your MPT library include procedural rules, that is a sign that you should include procedural rules in your MPT answer.

If you need to include a procedural rule or standard in your analysis, it will likely be the first rule in your analysis section, with the other rules of general applicability following after. Here is an excerpt of a trial standard from a criminal trial brief. (This passage uses MPT citation style; on the MEE and other bar essays you do not need to use citations.):

> When reviewing a Rule 29 motion for judgment of acquittal, a court's review "is strict, and a jury's guilty verdict should not be overturned lightly." *United States v. Pizano* (8th Cir. 2005). "In reviewing a claim

of insufficiency of the evidence, [the court] must determine whether, after viewing the evidence in the light most favorable to the prosecution, *any* rational trier of fact could have found the essential elements of the crime beyond a reasonable doubt." *Jackson v. Virginia* (U.S. Sup. Ct. 1979).

When writing your analysis, give as much attention to your procedural rules as you do to the rest of your rules of general applicability.

Funnel and Roadmap

As you present your rules of general applicability, you should move from the rules that are most general to the rules that are most specific to the facts of your case. This process is called **narrowing the scope of the rule**. The most general rule is the procedural standard, so if you have one, start with that. The next most general rule is the rule that governs your substantive issue. If that rule has sub-parts, such as **elements or factors,** list those next.

If you have an elements test, and any of those elements don't apply to the facts of your case and therefore will be excluded from your analysis, mention that exclusion in your funnel. Likewise, if an element applies but the analysis is simple, you can dispose of that element quickly with a one-sentence analysis. By the end of your funnel, you will end up with the narrow rule or set of rules that you will apply in your analysis.

If your analysis has multiple parts, the end of your funnel should include a roadmap that announces the order of the rest of your analysis. If the end of your funnel contains a rule with multiple elements, your roadmap should describe the outcome of each element. Alternatively, if your quirky boss instructed you to write your analysis using a particular organization, describe that organization in your roadmap.

Here is a template for a roadmap that you might find useful when you are writing under pressure. This roadmap template of an elements test includes the conclusions for any sub-issues that are still at issue in your analysis **and the order in which you handle the sub-issues.** Note that your roadmap does not need to be long (and shouldn't be).

> To prevail on _____, the plaintiff must show (1) _____ and (2) _____. CITE. Here, neither of these elements are met.

Let's fill in this template to see how it works. Below is an excerpt from an office memo that you are writing for your supervisor about whether the plaintiff can prevail on a negligence claim against your client, the defendant store owner. This example uses MPT citation style to cite sources from the fictional jurisdiction of Rhode Hampshire.

> To prevail on a nuisance claim, the plaintiff must show (1) that the defendant used his property unreasonably and (2) that unreasonable use created an obnoxious condition for the plaintiff neighbor. *Mitchell v. Diamond* (R.H. Ct. App. 2018). Here, neither of these elements is met.

This roadmap template works well if you plan to discuss all of the elements in a branching analysis. But what if you plan only to discuss one or two of them, because the others are so obviously met (or not) that you can address them in one or two sentences? In that situation, you'll summarily dispose of the undisputed elements between your elements test and your roadmap. Here's an example:

> To prevail on a negligence claim, the plaintiff customer must show (1) that the defendant owed a duty to the plaintiff, (2) that the defendant breached his duty to the plaintiff, (3) that the breach of duty caused the plaintiff (4) to suffer an injury. *State v. Terrence*, R.H. Sup. Ct. 2008. Here, elements 1 and 3 are undisputed. All store owners owe customers like the plaintiff a duty to protect them from unreasonably dangerous conditions. *Id.* And the snake unquestionably caused the plaintiff to drop his package of ice cream when the plaintiff encountered it on Aisle 7. Because the elements of duty and causation are not at issue, the only remaining elements of negligence at issue are breach of duty and harm. The plaintiff will likely not prevail on a negligence claim because (A) the store owner did not breach her duty to the plaintiff when the snake entered the store and (B) the plaintiff did not suffer actual harm from his encounter with the snake.

After summarily discarding two of the four elements of negligence in your funnel, you could write an accurate roadmap that previewed the only two elements that your analysis would address in detail. This version of a roadmap presents the elements along with the conclusions *at the same time*. Presenting the elements with their conclusions is a different, equally valid way to write a roadmap.

However you write your roadmap, be sure to **present your elements in the order that you will discuss them** in your subsections. And after you conclude your roadmap, begin your first subsection with **a strong conclusion heading** addressing your first element. Some writers believe that they do not need to write a conclusion heading after writing a roadmap because doing so seems repetitive. They are wrong.

Rule Examples

A rule example (or "rule illustration") describes how a court applied a rule of general applicability to the facts of a particular case to reach an outcome. Rule examples describe the facts, reasoning, and outcome from a precedent case. Rule examples can help readers understand rules of general applicability by showing how courts applied those rules to real facts.

Rule examples are most helpful, though, for analogies—drawing comparisons between the example and your facts—and distinctions—showing contrasts between the example and your facts. You can use the facts from your rule examples to show the reader how a rule of general applicability does or does not apply to your case.

Here is a rule of general applicability from the fictional jurisdiction of Rhode Hampshire using MPT citation style:

> Taking a large, valuable livestock animal, whose fiber has significant commercial value, can be a Class H felony. *State v. Bosley* (R.H. Sup. Ct. 2005).

Here is a rule example that uses the *Bosley* opinion to explain the rule:

> For example, the *Bosley* court upheld a felony conviction for taking a 600-pound muskox whose fiber could be harvested annually and sold for approximately $1,000. *Id.* The court reasoned that the muskox was close in size to the large animals named in the statute—horses, cows, and bulls—and that the muskox had high commercial value because its fiber was worth $150 per pound. *Id.*

You can tell that a paragraph is a rule example paragraph because it begins with the **transition phrase** "For example." You will learn more about transition words and phrases in Part G of this appendix.

In the above rule example paragraph, the writer uses the facts of *Bosley* to explain the rule, making it easier for the reader to understand why, for example, the rule mentioned the word "fiber." It turns out, a livestock animal can be raised not just for its meat, but also for its hair.

When you write rule example paragraphs, begin them in one of two ways:

> (1) **One Paragraph**: Begin the paragraph by stating the rule of general applicability in the first sentence. The next sentence in the paragraph then begins with the default phrase "For example," and the rest of the paragraph explains the rule. This works best when your rule of general applicability does not need to be narrowed in scope to fit your facts.

(2) **Two Paragraphs:** The first paragraph is a rule of general applicability paragraph, one that funnels from broad to narrow, ending with a final sentence providing the rule that you are about to explain. The second paragraph is a rule example paragraph; the first sentence begins with the default phrase "For example"; then it provides the holding of the case you are using as an example. By stating the holding first, you are explaining what the case is about and why you are including it. Next, include relevant facts (and only relevant facts) from the example case. The relevant facts are the ones that helped determine the case's outcome.

Here is a rule example paragraph of the second type that uses informal MPT citation style. Presume that the first paragraph ended with this rule of general applicability: To be "substantial," an interference with the plaintiff's use of her property must involve "more than slight inconvenience or petty annoyance." *Watts.*

> For example, in *Watts,* the court held that a manufacturing plant substantially interfered with a plaintiff's house. *Watts.* The plant installed machinery and air conditioning equipment that ran continuously for "6 or 6½ days each week" and created vibrations that caused the house's foundation to sink by two inches, molding to pull away from the walls, dishes to clatter, and the chimney to pull away from the walls. *Id.*

Note that this rule example paragraph opens with the default phrase "For example," gives the holding of the example case as a topic sentence, and then provides the relevant facts that determined the case's outcome.

To make writing rule examples under pressure easier, here's a template you can use:

> For example, in case _____, the court held B because X and Y happened.

Although you will use rule example paragraphs throughout your MPT tasks, you will not write them in your MEE essays. After all, you do not have case law at hand to gather the amount of information required to write this detailed law. Instead, when writing the MEE or other bar essays, you apply the rules of general applicability that you write from memory to fact patterns, pairing rules with facts (rather than analogizing to precedent cases).

Synthesis

Once you have gathered together the legal authorities that you will apply to your facts, synthesize these legal authorities into a meaningful rule that aligns with the facts of your case. You synthesize law when you combine together rules from multiple preexisting legal authorities (such as the different legal authorities in your MPT library or different black letter rules from your subject-matter outlines).

Here's an MPT example: Imagine an MPT library containing a statute and two cases that apply the statute to specific facts. The statute and cases might each describe the law a bit differently, but they are all getting at the same legal principles. You need to synthesize the statute and cases to describe those common legal principles to your reader. Synthesized rules will be rules of general applicability that you can both apply and illustrate. Providing a strong rule synthesis increases the likelihood that your reader will understand the rule and your analysis, and makes it easier to apply the rule to your facts.

On the MEE, though, you will synthesize from your memory rather than from printed legal authorities in your exam packet. The law that you have memorized is your "library" for the MEE or other bar essays. Your essay rule passage will probably be shorter than a rule passage would normally be in an office memo, but you should still write enough legal rules to apply to your fact pattern. (After you write your application section on the bar essay, return to your rule passage and update it with any law that you might have remembered.)

E. Application Passages

In the application section of your analysis, explain to your reader how the rules you wrote apply to your facts to support your conclusion. You will need to repeat some of the facts from your facts section and some of the law from your rule section, but you do not need to repeat all of the rules and facts.

🔥 Hot Tip

In professional legal documents, you usually write fact sections. Office memos and briefs have document parts with headings for statements of facts. However, **the MPT usually instructs you *not* to write a fact section.** Pay close attention to this instruction; indeed, you should look for it. And, on the MEE, you do not write a fact section at all.

In your application, your job is to align the key law with the key facts of your case. To write a strong application passage, you should pair key law with key facts in every sentence, drawing connections between the law and the facts from the beginning of your application to the end. You might feel like you are over-explaining the connections between law and facts, but you probably aren't. If you are in doubt, over-explain.

When the rule of general applicability aligns directly with the facts of your case, your job is easy. You can state the rule and apply it directly to your facts. But sometimes there is a gap between the rule of general applicability and your facts. When that is the case, you must use rule examples to draw comparisons between or distinctions from your facts and the facts of the precedent case you used as a rule example.

Comparisons (or analogies) show how your case is similar to a precedential case; distinctions show how your case is dissimilar to a precedential case. If you want to draw a comparison, show how the facts of your case align with the facts of the precedential case. If you want to draw a distinction, show how the facts of your case do not align with the facts of the precedential case.

When you write an application passage, transition from your rule passage to your application passage by starting a new paragraph. Begin that paragraph with the transition word "Here." "Here" is clear, and it is short. You can't go wrong with "Here." Decide now to use "Here" on your MPT and MEE, and you won't have to think about it later. Every time you write a practice MPT or MEE, use "Here" to transition from rule passage to application. Doing so will make this default transition into a helpful habit.

After writing the word "Here" at the beginning of your application paragraph, write the claim that your application paragraph is proving. Many people forget topic sentences in application paragraphs, including some people who prepare the MPT point sheets and MEE sample answers. But you should write them. The claim is the entire point of your paragraph. You want your reader to know the point of your paragraph after the first sentence. That way, the rest of the paragraph can prove that claim by showing how the law and facts work together to prove it.

You might have a follow-up application paragraph (or more) that does *not* begin with the default word "Here." You don't need that transition word in later application paragraphs because you have already transitioned to your case from the law. But you might use a different default transition word like "Next" or "However."

Here is an example of an application paragraph that you might see in an MPT or MEE answer:

> Here, the "whole situation" shows that DEC unreasonably used its
> property as a de facto alligator refuge given the Perrys' residential use
> of their property. There is evidence to suggest that DEC deliberately
> created and maintained an environment that attracts wild alligators.
> The alligators now use DEC's property as a base from which to invade
> the Perrys' property.

This application paragraph begins with the default word "Here." Then, it states
the claim that the paragraph will prove: "that DEC unreasonably used its property as a de facto alligator refuge" under the law. Then, the paragraph applies
law to facts to prove that claim. The entire paragraph serves the purpose of
proving that topic sentence.

Another default application paragraph is the analogy paragraph. If you are
comparing your case favorably to another, that paragraph begins with the
default word "Like." If you are trying to distinguish another case from your
own, begin the paragraph with the default word "Unlike."

Here is an example of an analogy paragraph that you might see in an MPT
answer (analogies are uncommon in MEE essays):

> Like the geese in *Andrews*, the alligators are not naturally occurring on
> DEC's property and have been reduced to DEC's possession. DEC went
> further than the defendant in *Andrews* by bringing the alligators onto
> the property rather than just luring them there with food, water, and
> companionship. In addition, DEC deliberately created an environment
> in which alligators would both flourish and stay put: It created artificial
> ponds, which it stocked with fish and surrounded with rabbits.

This analogy paragraph begins with the default word "Like." Then, it states the
claim that the paragraph will prove by favorably comparing the fact pattern
with the precedent case *Andrews*. The rest of the paragraph proves this claim
by comparing facts from the precedent case to facts from the fact pattern and
explaining why the similarities are legally significant.

F. Conclusions to End an Analysis

The final step in writing your C-RAC is to write your conclusion(s). Your
conclusion should succinctly state the legal outcome when you apply the
relevant law to your determinative facts. You learned how to write a conclusion
in Section A of this chapter. What you need to learn now is where to write your
conclusions to end your analysis.

On the MPT, if you are writing an office memo, then you will have a document part labeled "Conclusion" that follows the document part labeled "Analysis." In the Conclusion, you will put your brief answers from the beginning of your memo.

But, in legal writing, an analysis section *also* needs to conclude. This is where things get more complicated. Do you need a separate conclusion section within your analysis section? After all, the acronym is C-RAC, isn't it? Should you label your conclusion section inside your analysis section?

The answer is, you do what your boss wants. On the MPT and the MEE, you need a conclusion paragraph that is set off with transition words that indicate a conclusion, e.g., "In conclusion." Thus, if you have a single-issue analysis, you will only have to write one conclusion paragraph. If you have a multi-issue analysis, you will have to write more than one conclusion, one for each issue.

On the MPT (not the MEE), at the end of an analysis section, write a single conclusion paragraph that ties all of the other conclusions together. Thus, on the MPT, you might write multiple conclusions: one at the end of each subsection of your analysis and one at the end of your analysis as a whole. And then, after you conclude your analysis, you will have an entire new document part titled "Conclusion" in which you will put your conclusion for your task, which can be one sentence. That's a lot of conclusions, yes. But you want to be sure that your quirky boss sees them all.

When you write your conclusion, start a new paragraph, unless your boss or court rules specifically instruct you not to. Begin your conclusion paragraphs with the phrase "In conclusion."

On the MEE, each of your numbered prompts (which you should rewrite as a conclusion heading) begins a C-RAC. The final paragraph of each C-RAC should be a conclusion paragraph, even if it is only one sentence long. Your conclusion paragraph should begin with the phrase "In conclusion." It should summarize the main rule and pertinent facts that led to your conclusion.

Similarly, on the MPT, each subsection of your application will have a conclusion paragraph. Each conclusion paragraph should begin with the phrase "In conclusion." Each of your conclusion paragraphs should summarize the main rule and pertinent facts that conclude your analysis.

G. Small-Scale Organization (Paragraphs and Sentences)

One of the challenges of bar writing is the time constraint. As a lawyer, you will also face time constraints in your work. Time constraints make you feel that you don't have time to write in a way that is easy to read and understand. But you do, at least somewhat. The strategies you will learn in this section will not only help you write fast and well on the bar exam, they will help you do so in your legal practice.

Use Default Writing Structures

Lawyers use certain default document structures, sentences, phrases, and even words to signal meaning quickly when they write. These defaults allow lawyers to communicate quickly and accurately, both as writers and as readers.

As readers, lawyers expect writing defaults. They even prefer writing defaults. They prefer encountering what they expect to encounter in the legal documents that they read. They don't want to spend their readerly energy decoding unexpected language.

As writers, lawyers use defaults not only because other lawyers expect to read them, but also because defaults help lawyers to write faster. By using defaults, lawyers don't have to spend writerly energy coming up with new ways to say the same thing.

◊ Hot Tip

This appendix provides prescriptive writing instruction to use under constrained writing conditions. The bar exam is a constrained writing situation — you have a short time to write your MPT tasks or MEE essays. But you will face time constraints and other constraints throughout your career, and you will also face readers who expect to read these default words. They are, in the end, part of the language lawyers use in practice, not just on the bar exam. Thus using default structures and words is not only a **legal writing skill** and a **test-taking skill** but also a **lawyering skill**.

The default structure that you are most familiar with is C-RAC. Legal readers expect to read it, and therefore they expect you, as a writer, to use it. But this expectation is a good thing because you have a default structure that you can turn to again and again when you need to communicate legal analysis. You don't have to create a new structure every time you write. Learn C-RAC and then rely upon it.

Other default structures include ones that you learned earlier in this appendix about how to write about the law: presenting the rules from the most general to the most specific (i.e., from broad to narrow), using subsections when doing a branching analysis, and using a funnel to convey rules that apply to a branching analysis.

Use Paragraphs and Topic Sentences

When writing for the bar, use one paragraph per topic, even if the paragraph is short. And begin each paragraph with a strong topic sentence. This organization will make it easier for the graders to give you points. Let's learn a little more about paragraphs and topic sentences.

Paragraphs in legal documents can have different purposes. In documents that use C-RAC, some paragraphs present the law: these are the paragraphs in rule passages. Some apply the law to the facts: these are the paragraphs in the application passages. What all paragraphs have in common is that they contain a single idea introduced by a topic sentence.

A topic sentence (1) appears at the beginning of a paragraph, (2) conveys the purpose of the paragraph it introduces, and (3) situates the paragraph within the document.

You should write paragraphs that contain only one kind of information—rule, or rule example, or application—and then use topic sentences to convey the kind of information that is in your paragraph. Using this default organization will make writing paragraphs easier for you and reading those paragraphs easier for your audience.

When you read sample answers for the MPT and MEE, you will not necessarily see strong topic sentences. However, *you* should write them. Building the habit of writing strong topic sentences will serve you well in practice. And, as we just told you, strong topic sentences will make it easier for your exam grader to give you more points.

Use Default Transition Words

Legal readers expect certain types of paragraphs to begin with certain transition words. Here is a list of some transition words. You have learned about some of these already, but we will review them again now:

- In general (to indicate a rule of general applicability)
- For example (to indicate a rule example)
- Here (to indicate a shift from rule to application)
- In conclusion (to indicate a shift from application to conclusion)

Default transition words, such as the words above, guide you and your reader through your legal analysis. Other transition words indicate comparison:

- Like
- Unlike
- By contrast

Here's an example:

"By contrast, the court in *Anderson* held ..."

To indicate direction changes:

· But
· However

Here's an example:

"However, if the plaintiff relied upon the actions of the defendant ..."

To indicate exceptions:

· Although

An example:

"Although most jurisdictions hold that ..."

Get used to using these default words to indicate these typical legal writing transitions. If you have the default words at your fingertips, you will write faster.

H. Citation on the MPT

On the MPT, you will not use *Bluebook* citation style. Instead, you will use an informal citation style that the MPT itself uses in its legal authorities. However, on the MPT, you *must* cite your legal authorities unless your task documents tell you not to. On the MPT, case citations include only the case name, the court abbreviation, and the year (the final two appear in parentheses). For more detailed instruction on MPT citation style, see Chapter 4, Practice the MPT.

Here is an example of a case in MPT citation style:

In the Matter of Devonia Rose (Olympia Sup. Ct. 2004).

MPT citation style also includes short forms and *id*. (See Chapter 4 for more information.)

On the MEE, you do not need to cite authorities at all. Thus you do not need to worry about citation. But on the MPT, you do need to cite sources. Here are some guidelines for how to write faster while incorporating citations into your writing.

While you write your schematic, you need to write your citations as you write your law. This style of writing is called "cite while you write." In practical legal writing in which you must use precise *Bluebook*-style citations, we suggest citing while you write by placing accurate shorthand citations in-text as you go and backfilling the precise citations later.

On the MPT, the MPT citation style is so simple that your accurate shorthand citation style is your final citation style. You need to learn the MPT citation style now, before you take the MPT, so that you can seamlessly cite while you write. When citing while you write, you might choose not to italicize case names because it interrupts your flow. That's fine; in the grand scheme of legal citations, italics are not that important, and you can add them later if you have time.

What you definitely do *not* want to do is waste time hunting down citations at the end of your exam while time is running down. To learn how to write MPT citation style, see Chapter 4, Practice the MPT.

Appendix 2

Legal Reading under Pressure

This appendix teaches techniques for reading law under time pressure so that you can use what you've read to complete a legal writing task. This appendix focuses particularly on the kinds of legal authorities that MPTs and other performance tests usually demand you to read under pressure: judicial opinions, statutes, and regulations. But the principles will often apply to other kinds of legal authorities.

A. Read Like a Lawyer, Not a Student

Lawyers usually read law so that they can **do something with what they've read**—write a brief, argue a motion, advise a client, revise a contract, and so on. And lawyers usually know what questions they are trying to answer as they research and read law—What are the elements of adverse possession in Ohio? Under what circumstances have employees given proper FMLA notice to their employers via email? Do people who operate haunted houses in Georgia owe a special duty to their customers? And so on.

When lawyers are reading law under time pressure, they generally have a clear purpose—to find rules and examples that they can use to complete lawyering tasks. Lawyers also read the law to keep up with developments in their areas of expertise, but that kind of reading is usually not done under pressure. (Lawyers might also read law for fun, but that kind of legal reading is beyond the scope of this book.)

Students, on the other hand, often read the law to prepare for law school classes or exams. If you are a recent law school graduate preparing for the bar exam, this is the kind of reading that you likely have done most recently. The purpose of that reading is to learn an area of law to prepare for the task of participating in a class session or answering exam questions correctly. The scope of student reading is broader—students can't focus only on the legal authorities that address certain legal questions because they don't know yet what those questions will be. Students need to read to be prepared to answer or discuss *any* legal questions that arise from their reading. And they need to use what they've read to build up their knowledge of the subject matter, mentally organizing new knowledge so that it fits with pre-existing knowledge.

If you are reading law to perform a lawyering task—whether in practice or on the MPT—you need to read like a lawyer, not a student. And that begins with having a clear understanding of what kind of information you are looking for in the authorities that you read.

🔥 Hot Tip

In real lawyering, you must skim. There are just too many words in the legal authorities that you will use. **On the MPT, don't skim.** The law on the MPT is tightly edited, and most of it will be useful to you. Annotate as you read and look for legal tests, rules about legal tests, and examples of courts applying legal tests. If there is a rule in the case law or statutes that you do not use in your application, chances are you should be using it. Go back to the facts, and look for how the law might apply to your MPT's facts.

B. Identify Your Specific Reading Purpose

Reading law can be slow going, no matter how skilled you are at it, and knowing what you're looking for as you're reading can limit how many times you must read a particular authority.

On the MPT, you'll know the legal issue or issues of your task by the time you finish reading the task memo. At the very least, you'll know the issues in general terms. You'll also know what you're supposed to do with what you read—either figure out the best answer to a legal question (in analysis-to-conclusion documents) or find the best support for a predetermined legal conclusion (in conclusion-to-analysis documents).

Here are some examples of specific reading purposes:

- In the State of Franklin, could a seven-foot-tall fence on a residential street be a nuisance? If so, under what conditions?
- Do the Model Rules of Professional Conduct allow lawyers to amend their retainer agreements to require binding arbitration for fee disputes? If so, under what conditions?
- What is required to successfully request a Yellowstone National Park visitor list under the federal Freedom of Information Act?

These look and sound a lot like "issues" that a supervisor might ask you to investigate or research questions that a client might pose to you. That's because they are.

Let's suppose we are trying to answer the first research question, about tall fences in Franklin. What will we be looking for during our legal reading? Here are some things:

- A definition of "nuisance" under Franklin law.
- The circumstances under which a fence can be a nuisance.
- A legal test that courts use to figure out if a particular fence is a nuisance.
- A case in which a court held that a fence was a nuisance.
- A case in which a court held that a fence was not a nuisance.

Before you invest time in reading legal authorities, know what your specific reading purpose is and what you're looking for. Doing so will enable you to focus your reading energy on the parts of your legal reading that matter most, like applicable legal tests and examples of courts applying those tests.

C. Look for Legal Tests

When reading law (particularly on the MPT), your primary goal is to find the legal test or tests that apply to your particular facts. A legal test is one kind of rule. A legal test is a rule that, if it could be applied directly to the facts of your case, would resolve your legal issue. Other rules might help define terms in a legal test or describe exceptions to the legal test. You can think of a legal test as the most important black letter rule that governs any particular legal issue. Here are some examples of legal issues and their corresponding legal tests:

Issue	Legal Test
In the State of Franklin, could a seven-foot-tall fence on a residential street be a nuisance? If so, under what conditions?	A private nuisance occurs when a person unreasonably uses her own property in a way that creates an obnoxious condition for her neighbor.
What is required to successfully request a Yellowstone National Park visitor list under the federal Freedom of Information Act?	The federal Freedom of Information Act requires all requests to be in writing, to reasonably describe the records sought, and not be precluded by one of FOIA's exemptions or exclusions.
How do you prove that the owner of a haunted house attraction in Franklin has met its heightened duty to provide adequate personnel and supervision to its guests?	To determine whether the owner of a haunted house has met its heightened duty to provide adequate personnel and supervision to its guests, courts consider the number of employees per attraction, whether employees supervised guests in areas where they were likely to become scared, and whether employees were instructed about what to do if a guest was injured.

If you apply a legal test to the facts of your case, then you will reach a conclusion about a legal issue.

Simple Tests

A simple test is a test that doesn't have any sub-parts (no factors or elements). It is a rule with a straightforward yes or no answer. (Note: these are rare.)

Let's consider this specific reading purpose: In the State of Franklin, could a seven-foot-tall fence on a residential street be a nuisance? If so, under what conditions?

Suppose that this is our legal test: a seven-foot-tall fence built in a residential neighborhood is *always* an unreasonable use of property, one that creates an obnoxious condition for a neighbor.

We would know that the answer to the first question is "yes" and that the answer to the second question is "all conditions" and that we have satisfied our specific reading purpose. The test is a simple one.

When you spot a legal test that applies to your legal task, write it down. On the MPT, type the test right into your schematic as soon as you spot it (and circle it on your test booklet, annotating it as a test). As you continue reading the law, you'll add more information about the test to your schematic.

Each legal issue tends to have one legal test; thus, each C-RAC will have a legal test. Almost all legal tests will require further explanation—more rules that explain how they work and examples of when the test has been applied in the past. Some tests, though, are not so simple as the one in our example. Instead, they have multiple parts to keep track of.

Elements Tests

Many legal tests have multiple parts to them. One example of a test that has multiple parts is an elements test. (Another is a factor test, which we'll talk about in the next section.) An **elements test** is a rule that contains elements. An **element** is one part of a rule that *must* be proven in order for a claim to succeed. In other words, each element is a requirement. Legal authorities usually explicitly state the elements that make up elements tests.

Keeping to our specific reading purpose about fences and nuisance, we find this rule in case law: "A spite fence is a fence that serves no useful purpose for its owner and is maintained for the sole purpose of aggravating a neighbor."

This rule is an elements test with two elements. But how can you tell that it is a test? And how can you tell that it has two elements?

Sometimes elements tests can be easy to spot because the judicial opinion numbers the parts of the test, like this:

> A spite fence is a fence that (1) serves no useful purpose for its owner and (2) is maintained for the sole purpose of aggravating a neighbor.

Reading a legal test with numbered parts is helpful because you know at a glance what the parts of the test are. Numbered elements tests practically jump off of the page at you. And, you also know that will need to keep reading to learn more about how to satisfy each element.

Sometimes elements tests have multiple parts to them, and not only are those parts not numbered in the opinion, but the division of the elements can be fuzzy. In those situations, you not only have to identify the parts yourself, but you have to figure out how the case law typically divides the elements. Here's an example. Try to divide this rule into elements:

> The federal Freedom of Information Act requires all requests to be in writing, to reasonably describe the records sought, and not be precluded by one of FOIA's exemptions or exclusions.

How many elements did you decide that this rule has? Three? Four? The first element is that the request be in writing. The second element is that the request reasonably describe the records being sought. And then the third element is that the request not be precluded by one of FOIA's exemptions or exclusions. Or, do you think you could break that last element up into two—one about exemptions and one about exclusions? Sure! But before you do, keep reading case law about the test to see how courts have divvied up the parts. If you read two (or more) opinions that apply that test and both of them address FOIA exemptions separately from FOIA exclusions, then that indicates that you should break up this test into four parts. (Note: on the MPT, you might only have one case, and you should divide the elements the way that one case does.)

Once you've broken up your test into its elements, you'll need to keep reading the case law to figure out how courts apply the test. But before you do, **write "TEST" in all caps on your MPT materials** so that you can find it again easily. Then, **type the test into your schematic** because you will likely use the test to organize your analysis.

Factor Tests

A **factor** is a fact or condition that may *contribute* to a particular outcome but does not *determine* the outcome. (You can think of a factor as a dimmer, in contrast to an element's on/off switch.) A **factor test** is a rule that contains factors. Factor tests are also sometimes called **balancing tests**, **weighing tests**, and **totality-of-the-circumstances tests**. Regardless, when legal writers apply factor tests, they don't have to prove all of the factors. Instead, they analyze the merits of different factors and then, *considering the factors together*, they draw conclusions.

Here is an example of a factor test. Read it and identify the factors.

> To determine whether the owner of a haunted house has met its heightened duty to provide adequate personnel and supervision to its guests, courts consider the number of employees per attraction, whether employees supervised guests in areas where they were likely to become scared, and whether employees were instructed about what to do if a guest was injured.

You might have noticed that this factor test didn't use the word "factor" anywhere. So how do we even know that it's a factor test? Because the test doesn't use language of requirement, like "must" or "shall" or "requires," and because the test does list some items to "consider." Verbs like "consider" or "weigh" or "examine" often indicate factor tests. With that reading tip in mind, this test describes three "considerations." In other words, this test has three factors: (1) the number of employees per attraction, (2) whether employees supervised guests in areas where they were likely to become scared, and (3) whether employees were instructed about what to do if a guest was injured.

🔥 Hot Tip

> When you notice an elements test or a factor test while you're reading, flag it with a helpful annotation. For example, you might write "factor test for heightened duty" or "elements test for FOIA request." Writing a short description like this will make your annotations more useful because you'll know at a glance what the words of the opinion are about. If you only highlight, you just know that the words are important; you'll have to read the language again to remember why you highlighted them.

D. Look for Examples in Case Law

In addition to looking for tests and rules when you read, also look for examples that you can compare or contrast to your facts. A useful example will have these features:

- It will describe when a court applied your legal test to a set of facts.
- That set of facts will be similar to your facts.
- You can tell whether the court held that the legal test was satisfied or not satisfied.

You will use these examples to draw analogies and distinctions in your legal analysis. These analogies and distinctions will help prove that the conclusions in your legal document are the correct conclusions.

E. Connect Together What You Read

Noticing legal tests as you read is an essential legal reading skill. But spotting legal tests isn't enough. You need to understand the law so that you can apply it to your facts in writing, well enough to convince a skeptical audience who needs the law explained to her. Thus when reading law for the purpose of completing a legal task, you also need to be able to understand the test thoroughly enough so that you can explain it to a reader. Your explanation could include a lot of details, if the test is complicated. Or it could include just another sentence or two, if the test requires little explanation to be understood and applied.

One way you'll know how elaborate your own explanation of a test needs to be is by how elaborate the explanation of the test is *in the law that you read*. A judicial opinion can not only provide the law that you need to complete your task, but it can also serve as an example of how thoroughly you need to describe your test. Let's pick up our FOIA example.

Because FOIA is a statute, we begin looking for a test in FOIA itself. On the MPT, relevant excerpts of FOIA would be provided to you; in real life, you would need to locate the relevant parts of FOIA yourself. Here are some parts of FOIA that are relevant:

- Statute: "[E]ach agency, upon any request for records which (i) reasonably describe such records and (ii) is made in accordance with published ... procedures to be followed, shall make the records promptly available to any person." 5 U.S.C. §552(a)(3)(A).
- Statute: The requirement to make records available does not apply to matters that are "personnel and medical files and similar files the disclosure of which would constitute a clearly unwarranted invasion of personal privacy." 5 U.S.C. §552(b)(6).

The first provision looks like a legal test for when an agency must give records to a person who requests them. So long as the request (1) reasonably describes the records and (2) follows the necessary procedures, like being in writing, the agency must release the records. But the second provision makes it look like an agency doesn't have to release records sometimes, even if those two requirements are met. Instead, the second provision says that the test doesn't apply to matters that are personnel related and medical files and similar files that would cause an unwarranted invasion of personal privacy. So which rule is right? Which one will get our client the visitor log from Yellowstone?

Both rules are right. And as a legal reader, you must recognize that both rules are right and fit them together in a way that makes sense. One way to fit our two rules from FOIA together is to think of the first as an "in general" rule and the second as an exception to that general rule. Like this:

> **In general**, agencies must make records promptly available to any person so long as the request reasonably describes the desired records and follows "published procedures" for making requests. 5 U.S.C. §552(a)(3)(A).

An exception to this general rule is that agencies do not have to provide "personnel and medical files and similar files the disclosure of which would constitute a clearly unwarranted invasion of personal privacy." 5 U.S.C. §552(b)(6).

Now we can see how the two rules fit together with one another. The bolded phrases show that the first rule is a general one, and the second rule is an exception to that general rule. We are starting to diagram the law.

We need to add more, though, because statutes alone rarely provide a complete picture of how a legal test works. Statutes are written in broad language designed to cover many factual scenarios. However, the language is often so broad that you cannot easily apply the language of the statute to your facts with confidence. Usually, the broad language of a statute is explained in more detail by regulations and case law. As you're reading case law related to a statute, look for the name or citation to the statute. Often that is a cue that that part of the case will describe how the statutes work in more detail.

◊ Hot Tip

> Many MPTs provide statutory provisions along with judicial opinions that apply those statutory provisions. The statutes will appear first in your legal library, and the opinions will follow. You should read the law in the order it's presented. Because MPT law is so tightly edited, the statutory provisions that you read are either the provisions that apply to your facts or the provisions that you need to know *don't* apply to your facts. After you read the statutory provisions, read the cases with those statutory provisions in mind and pay attention to any words from the statute that are defined by the opinions.

For our purposes, let's add these rules from a regulation, a U.S. Supreme Court case, and a circuit court case.

- "To the extent possible, requesters should include specific information … such as the date, title or name, author, recipient, subject matter of the record, case number, file designation, or reference number." 6 C.F.R. §5.3(b).
- "Similar files" contain "detailed Government records … which can be identified as applying to that individual." This includes information such as "place of birth, date of birth, date of marriage,

employment history, and … passport information." *U.S. Dep't of State v. Ray* (U.S. 1991).

- Once a file has been determined to be a personnel, medical file, or similar file, a court must balance that individual's right of privacy against the benefit to the public of opening up the agency action to the light of public scrutiny. *U.S. Dep't of State v. Ray* (U.S. 1991).

- "Similar files" under Exemption 6 should be read broadly and includes individuals' personal information in public records, even if that information is not embarrassing or otherwise intimate. *Daffee v. U.S. Dep't of Interior* (15th Cir. 2010).

- A newspaper reporter made a FOIA request for a list of people who had made purchases from the souvenir shop at Devil's Tower National Monument, which is operated by the National Park Service. FOIA denied her request under Exemption 6. The reporter sued the National Park Service, arguing that the denial was improper. The courts disagreed. The requested list was a "similar file" because it included individuals' personal information. Releasing this information would reveal not only the names of people who had visited Devil's Tower but also whether they had purchased items at the gift shop. The public benefit was minimal because the reporter planned to use the information to write an article about gift shop sales in Wyoming. On balance, individuals' right of privacy significantly outweighed any benefit to the public. *Daffee v. U.S. Dep't of Interior* (15th Cir. 2010).

Suppose that as we read the legal authorities, these rules stood out to us as potentially applicable to our specific reading purpose of determining whether we can use FOIA to get a list of visitor names from Yellowstone National Park. As we read, we typed them into our notes (or schematic) without thinking too hard about how the rules all fit together. But now let's think about them and add them to our diagram. The bolded phrases show how each rule relates to the ones preceding it.

> **In general**, agencies must make records promptly available to any person so long as the request reasonably describes the desired records and follows "published procedures" for making requests. 5 U.S.C. §552(a)(3)(A).

> **More specifically**, "[t]o the extent possible, requesters should include specific information … such as the date, title or name, author, recipient, subject matter of the record, case number, file designation, or reference number." 6 C.F.R. §5.3(b).

An exception to the general rule is that agencies do not have to provide "personnel and medical files and similar files the disclosure of which would constitute a clearly unwarranted invasion of personal privacy." 5 U.S.C. § 552(b)(6).

The phrase "similar files" is defined as "detailed Government records ... which can be identified as applying to that individual." This includes information such as "place of birth, date of birth, date of marriage, employment history, and ... passport information." *U.S. Dep't of State v. Ray* (U.S. 1991).

Furthermore, "similar files" under Exemption 6 should be read broadly and includes individuals' personal information in public records, even if that information is not embarrassing or otherwise intimate. *Daffee v. U.S. Dep't of Interior* (15th Cir. 2010).

For example, a list of people who made purchases at the gift shop of a National Monument was a "similar file" because it contained the names of individuals who had visited that National monument and also whether they had made purchases at its gift shop. *Daffee v. U.S. Dep't of Interior* (15th Cir. 2010).

Once a file has been determined to be a personnel, medical file, or similar file, **the next step** is for the court to balance that individual's right of privacy against the benefit to the public of opening up the agency action to the light of public scrutiny. *U.S. Dep't of State v. Ray* (U.S. 1991).

For example, writing an article about gift shop sales in Wyoming would confer little public benefit and was significantly outweighed by the privacy rights of the individuals whose names would be released if the government granted a reporter's request for a list of people who made purchases at the Devil's Tower National Monument gift shop. *Daffee v. U.S. Dep't of Interior* (15th Cir. 2010).

◊ Hot Tip

On the MPT, the legal authorities are tightly edited and there isn't much excess law. If you read more than two paragraphs of law about a legal topic that you haven't written about in your schematic, there's a good chance that legal topic should be part of your MPT answer. Revisit your facts to see if any correspond to the legal topic.

F. Techniques for Annotating MPT Law

On the MPT, you'll only have time for one thorough read of the legal authorities. You also won't be able to easily search for phrases you've already read, the way you might if you were reading a case on an online legal database. Because of this constraint, as you read the law, you should annotate it—and annotate it in a way that makes it easy to spot rules, examples, facts, or quotes that you think you'll need as you write your MPT answer. You can add to your schematic as you annotate.

Here are some techniques for annotating judicial opinions:

- Write a quick reverse outline in the margin as you read. Label the parts of the opinion that describe facts, law, and examples. And label the parts that apply the law to the facts of the case. These labels will make it easy for you to quickly refer back to different parts of the opinion if you need to.
- When you encounter a test, write "TEST" next to it. You should also type the test into your schematic, but the annotation will help you quickly refer back to it if you need to.
- When you read a useful example, note whether it is a "YES" example (the legal test was not met) or a "NO" example (the legal test was not met). The MPT often includes examples within cases—summaries of cases that you haven't read—that it expects you to use in your answer. Labeling examples as YES or NO examples will help you decide which examples to use to compare and contrast with your facts.

Here are some techniques for annotating statutes, regulations, court rules, etc.:

- Statutory provisions are usually written to work together with neighboring provisions. If you receive multiple statutory provisions, notice how they relate to each other. Are they equivalent sections, or are some sub-sections of others? For example, if you see a word in one section that is defined in another, draw a line connecting the two.
- Mark words that indicate relationships, like these: and, or, either, if, unless, when, not, only.
- Mark words that indicate requirement (must, shall, will) or permission (may).

Index